Alden Aaroe:
Voice of the Morning

Alden Aaroe:
Voice of the Morning

The Dietz Press
Richmond, Virginia

ISBN #   Hard Cover 0-87517-072-2
            Soft Cover   0-87517-073-0

I have at times in my life known at a given time that at that moment I was experiencing something unique, something that would perhaps never again be recaptured. For a moment I have stood and looked and locked into myself the scene, the person, the event, saying this goes into my library of memories.

These are good memories to have against a day when perhaps, and God forbid, the life may not be as sweet.

— Alden Aaroe, in a letter to his daughter, Anna Lou, in 1963.

Acknowledgments

Being a novice at book-writing, I am tempted, of course, to thank everyone who ever gave me a pat on the back, beginning with the North Carolina doctor who delivered me into this world.

In the interest of the reader, however, I will restrain myself.

My highest level of gratitude goes to the three delightfully charming women who provided the bulk of the material in this story of Alden Aaroe's life. They are Anna Lou Aaroe Schaberg, his daughter, Frances Perry Aaroe, his widow, and Edna Kirby Aaroe, his first wife. Each member of this triumvirate of storytellers was resourceful and cooperative, and without their help this book never would have been written.

I also am deeply grateful to several people who worked with Aaroe at WRVA Radio and shared their memories. They include John Tansey, Brick Rider, John Harding, Lou Dean and Tim Timberlake.

A word of thanks also goes to *Richmond Times-Dispatch* Executive Editor Alf Goodykoontz, who gave me permission to use the newspaper's computer system to write my book. I'm also indebted to the Times-Dispatch photographer Masaaki "Mac" Okada, who brought to life a number of old photographic negatives dating back to Aaroe's youth.

Finally, I want to salute the late William Roy Smith of Petersburg, who got this project off the ground and gave me the opportunity to be a part of it. I just wished Roy had lived to see the finished product.

Contents

Preface

Alden Aaroe did not invent the radio, nor did he hang the moon.

It only seemed that way to the legions of people who listened to Aaroe on Richmond's WRVA for nearly half a century.

WRVA hired Aaroe as a staff announcer in 1946. He was a gangling, 27-year-old veteran of World War II who had flown transport planes for the U.S. Army Air Forces out of a base in Teheran, Iran. He had contracted malaria during the war and when he arrived in Virginia's capital city he still was suffering from occasional flare-ups of the yellow fever.

Before the war, he had attended the University of Virginia, where he had shown promise as an actor for the Virginia Players. After four years of study in which his major was economics, he had to leave U.Va. without a diploma because his mother pulled the financial support plug and Alden was short of the academic requirements needed to graduate. Needing a steady paycheck, Alden took a job as an announcer for WCHV Radio in Charlottesville.

His rise to fame in Richmond radio began in 1956 when WRVA made Aaroe its voice of the morning. His plain-talking style and winsome personality quickly won over a flock of faithful listeners and he became Richmond's best-known radio personality.

At one time, Aaroe was ranked No. 1 on Richmond radio's ratings lists and his name also was the first one listed in the city's telephone book.

He did not stay first in the phone book, but he did stay No. 1 in the ratings until the final days of his WRVA career, which spanned six decades, from the 1940s to the 1990s.

In short, Alden Aaroe became a Richmond legend.

When he died of cancer at the age of 75 in the wee hours of the morning on July 7, 1993, his death was mourned by countless thousands of people whose lives had been touched by Aaroe's familiar voice coming out of their radios.

Writing a biography about a legend is never easy. There are too many stories to tell and too many bases to touch.

In writing this biography of Alden Aaroe, I attempted only to tell some of the stories and touch some of the bases.

By his own words, Aaroe led a wonderful life.

He also led a fascinating life, full of ups and downs, as these pages should reveal. He was 100 percent human being.

Near the end of his life, Alden Aaroe had a long telephone conversation with Andrew Willett, his grandson. Andrew was finishing up requirements for a bachelor's degree in architecture at Virginia Tech University in Blacksburg. Alden told his grandson to find a wooden beam on campus and to carve his initials there, so that years later Andrew could return to the place of his young manhood, find his initials and "laugh and cry and remember."

In a sense, Alden Aaroe spent his life carving his initials in many places, including the hearts of countless people.

Chapter One

Had the times been ordinary, he probably would have been born in the bucolic atmosphere of northwestern New Jersey, where his ancestors from Denmark had settled after getting off the boat at Ellis Island in the late 1800s.

When Alden Petersen Aaroe came into the world in the spring of 1918, however, the times were anything but ordinary. Events unfolding on the world's stage of history had a hand in selecting Alden Aaroe's birthplace. Instead of entering the world in rural New Jersey, he entered it in the citified atmosphere of the nation's capital, Washington, D.C., where his mother had been taken by the winds of war.

In the spring of 1917, one year before Aaroe's birth, President Woodrow Wilson announced the United States of America was joining forces with the Allies in the great war that had been waging in Europe since 1914. America's long-awaited entry into World War I disrupted the lives of many Americans, including a young couple from New Jersey named George Christian Aaroe and Anna Petersen Aaroe.

"The war to end all wars," as it was optimistically labeled, took George and Anna Aaroe to Washington in service of their country. George Aaroe was a U.S. Army officer who was involved in some way with the Army's fledgling aviation program in World War I. Anna Aaroe, an elementary schoolteacher, worked for the federal government in Washington in a job believed to have been secretarial.

So there in Washington, on May 5, 1918, Anna Aaroe gave birth to a son.

It is not known whether this baby boy had the loudest vocal chords in the nursery, but that would be a good guess, given the knowledge that this child's voice was to become the source of his livelihood.

At Alden Aaroe's birth, no one predicted he would become a radio announcer because in 1918 nobody knew what a radio station was. The first commercial radio station did not go on the air until 1920.

But radio was a coming force when Aaroe was born. After years of experimentation, inventors were fine-tuning the technology that would allow the radio to become an important part of everyone's life.

The history of the communications medium that was Alden Aaroe's passion goes back to the mid-1800s, when inventors scattered around the globe began seeking a way to send messages great distances without the use of a wire.

The first big breakthrough came in 1895 when Guglielmo Marconi, an Italian inventor, sent the first radio signals through the air by using electromagnetic waves to send telegraph code signals a distance of approximately a mile.

The world knew this magical invention as "Marconi's wireless."

Precisely when the human voice first was transmitted on a "wireless" long has been a matter of dispute. The honor generally is awarded to Reginald A. Fessenden, a Canadian-born physicist, who spoke by radio in 1906 from Brant Rock, on the Massachusetts coast near the historic town of Plymouth, to ships offshore in the Atlantic Ocean.

Another radio pioneer was Lee De Forest, an Iowa native who in 1907 received a U.S. patent for the vacuum tube, which became the key element in perfecting radio technology. De Forest also produced what is believed to have been the first radio program, a 1910 broadcast in New York City of a Metropolitan Opera performance by the legendary Enrico Caruso.

Despite this flurry of activity in the early years of the 20th Century, Alden Aaroe was born at a time when the radio was merely a clumsy gadget with great potential, like a human baby.

In the latter years of Aaroe's long career at Richmond's WRVA Radio, his colleagues sometimes quipped that Alden had been around since "Day One." In a sense, that was true, because Aaroe and commercial radio were born about the same time.

In 1920, when Aaroe was two years old, the first two commercial radio stations went on the air -- WWJ in Detroit and KDKA in Pittsburgh.

Although a case can be made for Detroit's WWJ being the first commercial radio station in the country, most people in the industry side with KDKA, which traces its roots to an experimental station that began operating in 1916 in Wilkinsburg, a Pittsburgh suburb.

Seven years after the birth of Alden Aaroe and five years after the birth of commercial radio, Richmond got its first radio station.

On the evening of Nov. 2, 1925, WRVA made its premiere broadcast from a small studio on Main Street with the aid of a 1,000-watt transmitter atop the roof of the tobacco company Larus & Brother's building at 22nd and Cary Streets. Thus was born the radio station that would make Alden Aaroe a household name in Richmond and throughout many parts of Virginia.

Before Aaroe and WRVA became a match made in radio heaven, however, he had a lot of growing up to do.

The growing up started in the town of Oxford in northwestern New Jersey, a few miles from the Delaware River and the Pennsylvania border, in a house on a 106-acre dairy farm owned by his maternal grandparents, Peter Madsen Petersen and Christeane Janny Petersen, both of whom had been born in Denmark.

That New Jersey dairy farm was where Alden went to live at a very early age. He spent the first six years of his life there, while his mother lived across the state in the town of Summit in the Jersey suburbs of New York City.

In Summit, Anna Aaroe taught sixth grade at Washington Elementary School and lived in an apartment. On weekends she caught a train to Oxford to be with her parents and her son.

Meanwhile, Alden's father, George, had dropped out of the picture.

George and Anna went their separate ways about the time World War I ended in November of 1918, when Alden was six months old. One of the saddest aspects of Alden Aaroe's life is that his father was a shadow figure.

Aaroe's cousin, Faye Jensen-Yeager, who lives in the New

Jersey farm house where Alden spent his early childhood years, recalls being told that Alden's parents separated shortly after he was born.

"George and Anna never divorced," said Mrs. Jensen-Yeager, whose mother was the sister of Alden's mother. "They just went their separate ways, and, to the best of my knowledge, never saw each other again."

The couple may have lived together briefly, however, in Alden's boyhood years. Aaroe's first wife, Edna Kirby Aaroe, remembers Alden saying he had faint memories of living in an apartment with his mother and father.

The hard truth, however, is that Alden Aaroe grew up fatherless. He never really knew his father, and as an adult he almost never talked about the man.

Consequently, not much is known about Alden Aaroe's father except for a few basic facts. George Aaroe was the son of Soren Aaroe and Jensina Jensen Aaroe, also people of Danish ancestry who had settled in Oxford, N.J. When their home in Oxford burned, Soren and Jensina moved to Metuchen, N.J.

George Aaroe met Anna Petersen through family. They were cousins. When they married is not known. What happened to him after they separated also is wrapped in mystery.

Alden's cousin Faye says that after George and Anna separated, George lived on Long Island at one point in his life. And in his later years he lived with his sister in Metuchen.

"It was in those later years," Faye said, "that I met George for the first time. He was a very charming man."

That Alden Aaroe grew into manhood without the benefit of a father surely explains why, when he became a father himself, he worked so hard to be an important part of his child's life.

"Daddy and I were very close," said Anna Lou Aaroe Schaberg, Aaroe's daughter and only child. "There was this strong bond between us. Everybody tells me I was the apple of his eye."

Although Alden Aaroe had no father to look up to in his

formative years, he did have a father figure: Peter Madsen Petersen, his maternal grandfather. Alden, the boy, spent his childhood years exploring the New Jersey dairy farm and tagging along after his grandfather, whom he called "Poppa."

When Aaroe became a grown man, he was the kind of fellow who loved to do handyman chores around the house. He loved to fix things and build things, just like Poppa, his grandfather.

Both grandparents had been born in Denmark and as children had come with their families to the United States in the late 1800s. Their families settled in Oxford, which had a large Danish population.

Aaroe was not one to be all wrapped up in his Danish heritage, but he did enjoy telling family stories that had been passed down from generation to generation.

One branch of his family had been weavers in Denmark for centuries. Years ago, the story goes, one of these weaving ancestors was asked to weave something special for the king of Denmark. The king even offered the use of the 300-year-old looms in his castle.

"I will be very happy to come to the castle to weave for you," Alden Aaroe's ancestor is said to have replied. "But I will bring my own looms, which are 500 years old."

Another family story is about the time an ancestor named Hans immigrated from Denmark and was greeted at Ellis Island by his brother Peter, who had several baskets of fresh vegetables in his wagon.

Seeing the vegetables, the hungry Hans, who had worn his best white shirt for his first day in America, reached into one basket and plucked what he thought was a red apple.

Unfortunately for Hans, it was not an apple, but a tomato. When he took a big bite, the tomato squirted all over the front of his finest white shirt. Hans had never seen a tomato before.

Alden's mother, whom everyone called Anna P., had been born and reared on the dairy farm of her Danish parents, who still were very Old World in their mannerisms and thoughts.

"My grandparents were very old-fashioned," Faye

Jensen-Yeager said.

"They were Lutherans and very religious. My grand-mother, Christeane, could describe God's throne and tell you exactly what God looked like."

Faye's and Alden's grandfather, Peter Petersen, was so hard of hearing that he was virtually deaf.

"You had to shout at him," Mrs. Jensen-Yeager said. "Late in life, he finally got a hearing aid and it opened up a whole new world for him. He never knew cars made a noise, and he heard birds singing for the first time."

On the other hand, Anna P. and her sister, Emma, were New World through and through.

"Looking back on the lives of Alden's mother and my mother," Faye Jensen-Yeager said, "I realize they were liberated women. They were outspoken, strong-willed, and very independent."

The original part of the Oxford farm house in which the Petersens' lived had been built before 1800. Over the years rooms were added, and whoever lived there around 1840 added a grand center hall and a large living room.

"When Alden was a boy living there, it was by no means a small farm house. It was a substantial home," said Mrs. Jensen-Yeager, who inherited the home from her mother, Emma, in 1975.

"Nevertheless, it was a farm in every sense of the word. It had 106 acres, a large barn, a smokehouse and a magnificent, three-seat outhouse -- two seats for adults and one for children."

When the time came for Alden to start first grade, his mother took him with her to Summit, where they lived in an apartment building. Anna P. had a great influence on his life, and, by all accounts, Alden worshipped his mother.

Anna wanted her son to attend Summit's schools, which had an excellent reputation. Furthermore, Summit was close to the cultural advantages of New York City. Taking the train, Anna and Alden could be in the city in about 45 minutes to see a play or visit a museum.

"Alden's mother was extremely serious about education," Mrs. Jensen-Yeager said. "She went into teaching right out of high school, and after she had been teaching for years, she went to college and got her bachelor's degree."

Anna P. was especially keen on vocabulary.

"She was always working on our vocabulary," Mrs. Jensen-Yeager said.

"If she heard us describe something as 'interesting,' she would say, 'Interesting says nothing. You should describe things as unusual, or remarkable.' "

About the time Alden left the farm to move to Summit with his mother, his cousin Faye, six years younger than Alden, moved with her family to the farm in Oxford from Detroit, Mich.

"I always said Alden was a farm boy who moved to the city and I was a city girl who moved to the farm," Faye said.

After moving to Summit, Alden and his mother frequently returned to Oxford by train for weekend visits.

"How I lived for those visits!" Mrs. Jensen-Yeager said. "As soon as Alden got there, he would grab my arm and say, 'Let's go for a walk.' In Detroit I had had many playmates my own age. But when we moved to the farm in Oxford, there weren't many children for me to play with. So when Alden came to visit, I was so happy. He was so much fun."

Alden and Faye were close during those years. "We were cousins, but we were more like brother and sister," she said.

Since Alden had spent his childhood years exploring every inch of the farm, he knew all the fun places to visit and all the fun things to do.

"He knew how to follow the rabbit tracks and the tracks of all the other animals," Mrs. Jensen-Yeager said. "He knew the names of all the birds and all the trees. And he could explain everything about nature in simple terms."

The countryside was their playhouse.

"We didn't have a lot of toys like kids today," Mrs. Jensen-Yeager said. "So we went all over the farm, including one forbidden place -- a big rock quarry behind the neighboring farm. That was our favorite place to go swimming and we always went there, even though the adults were constantly telling us not to go near the quarry."

Another favorite place was the barn, three stories tall.

"We loved to go into the barn, climb the ladder and jump into the hay," Mrs. Jensen-Yeager said. "Alden was a lot more reckless than I was. He would climb all to the third story and jump. The second was as high as I would go."

As an adult, Alden Aaroe developed quite a reputation among his family and friends as a practical jokester nonpareil.

His cousin Faye does not find this surprising, because the youthful Alden loved to play tricks on people.

"He had a wide streak of mischief in him," she said. "He was great one to play tricks. He's the one who taught me how to short-sheet a bed."

Faye never will forget the night at the farm when she had retired for the night in her bedroom, when suddenly the springs of her bed started making a terrifying racket. It was one of Alden's practical jokes.

"He had taken a spool of black thread, tied it to a tin cup and tied the cup to the bedsprings," she said. "When I got in bed he was out in the hallway with the spool of thread. When he tugged on the thread, it made the tin cup rattle against the springs."

Another Alden trick involved fox fire, the eerie luminescence of decaying wood that is created when wood is buried for a period of years and phosphorus is deposited.

"One night, Alden found some fox fire in a woodpile," she said. "I had a girlfriend spending the night with me, and not long after we had turned the lights out, we saw this strange green light moving around the room. It was Alden carrying the fox fire."

He also was a lad with a great imagination.

"One time," Mrs. Jensen-Yeager recalled, "he coaxed a doctor into giving him a handful of tongue depressors. Oh, the gadgets he made out of those tongue depressors!"

He also loved to play games. Alden the boy had a passion

for games that would burn all his life.

"He taught me to play gin rummy," Mrs. Jensen-Yeager said.

"And he loved to play croquet. At the farm we always left the croquet wickets set up all summer on a lawn under some trees. Alden was a vicious croquet player. Every time he got the chance, he would knock your ball to kingdom come, because he loved to win.

"On the other hand, if four of us cousins were playing croquet, Alden would team up with the one losing to help them catch up."

The adults in the family also had a great fondness for this inquisitive, mischievous, playful boy.

"My mother, who was a school principal, just adored him," said Mrs. Jensen-Yeager. "Everybody adored him. But he was not spoiled. His mother saw to that. She kept a tight rein on him."

When he entered Summit Junior High School for ninth grade, Alden became close friends with a boy named Karl Alfred. They remained the best of friends through the high school years and during college days at the University of Virginia in Charlottesville.

Dr. Karl Alfred grew up to become an orthopedic surgeon in Pepper Pike, Ohio, a suburb of Cleveland.

"In high school, Alden was a good actor who performed in several school plays," said Dr. Alfred. "He was a good student, but he didn't work to hard at it. And he picked up on playing the bass fiddle."

Romantically, his first true love was a Summit High School girl named Dorothea Morse.

"Dorothea was his high school sweetheart, and, as I recall, the only girl he ever dated in high school," Dr. Alfred said. "She was a wonderful girl. It was Alden's mother's wish that he would marry her. But it was not to be."

Dr. Alfred graduated from Summit High School in 1935, one year ahead of Alden, and went off to college to the University of Virginia.

The next year, in the fall of 1936, Alden entered U.Va.

"Alden always said I was the reason he chose Virginia," Dr. Alfred said. "I recommended the university to him, and he followed me down there."

Alden's first year in Charlottesville, he and Karl Alfred roomed together in Randall Hall, a campus dormitory. The next year they moved into Van Leer's rooming house with several other friends, including Mutt Womer, a champion boxer for the university.

At Mr. Jefferson's University, Aaroe chose economics for his major. He never graduated, but he had a lot of fun. He was not a fraternity man, but he attended many parties, and, like many college boys throughout the generations, was fond of strong drink.

One Sunday morning, after a particularly wild Saturday night, Alden was driving home across the Rivanna River. Looking down the river he saw elephants taking a bath. They were not pink elephants, but, still, the sight of elephants bathing in the Rivanna River is enough to make one wonder whether booze is taking its toll on one's brain. Alden promised himself to become more temperate in the consumption of spirits.

Later in the day, he learned that the elephants he had seen were real. The circus was in town, and the elephant trainers had taken their performers to the river.

His extracurricular passion, however, was not the party life, but rather the university's drama group, the Virginia Players, for which he performed in a number of plays.

He must have had some talent, based on a story Anna Lou tells.

In the winter of 1989, she and her husband, Robert W. "Bob" Schaberg, were vacationing at a resort in the Caribbean. One night at dinner, they were dining at the same table with Dr. Leonard Malis, then chairman of the department of neurosurgery at Mount Sinai Hospital in New York City.

When Dr. Malis learned that Anna Lou and Bob were from Richmond, he mentioned that he had been an undergraduate student at the University of Virginia in the late 1930s.

"Oh, so was my father!" Ann Lou said.

"Who was your father?" Dr. Malis said. "I might have known him."

"Alden Aaroe," she said.

Dr. Malis' face brightened.

"Of course I knew your father!" he said.

"We were both in the Virginia Players. He was an actor and I was a techy (production technician). And, let me tell you, whenever your father was on the stage, he dominated it. If Alden Aaroe were performing in a play, the rest of us boys made sure not to take our girlfriends, because they wouldn't pay attention to anybody but him."

When Anna Lou returned to Richmond, she recounted the story to Alden.

"I thought he was going to take flight," she said.

The conversation with Dr. Malis also confirmed in Anna Lou's mind what she had always believed: That her father as a young man was a tall, handsome, dashing fellow.

At the end of the 1937-38 school year, Karl Alfred left the university to enter medical school. After that, the two men seldom saw each other, but they kept up their friendship over the years.

"In the early years we saw each other in Summit in the summer months," Dr. Alfred said. "And in the fall of 1941, we got together and went to the Virginia-Yale football game in New Haven.

"Virginia's star was Bill Dudley and they had a great team that season. But they lost the game to Yale. It was the only game Virginia lost that season, and the only game Yale won."

By the fall of '40, Alden no longer was a student at U.Va. He had not completed the work necessary for a diploma, but his mother said four years was enough. He left school and took a full-time job as a staff announcer with Charlottesville radio station WCHV, which had given him a part-time job in 1938, when he was still a student.

His life had taken a romantic turn, too. He had found a new

love, a young woman who had grown up on a farm in Yancey Mills, a small community not far from Charlottesville in western Albemarle County.

Her name was Edna Louise Kirby.

When Alden met Edna, she was working at the F.W. Woolworth's store in downtown Charlottesville.

After they married, Alden was fond of borrowing a popular song title to say he had met his million-dollar baby in a five-and-ten-cent store.

Chapter Two

Alden Aaroe and Edna Kirby met on a blind date in Charlottesville in 1940. At the time, Alden was living in a rooming house and employed at radio station WCHV as a staff announcer. In 1938, while still a student, the station had given him a part-time job doing a five-minute news show five nights a week. His part-time salary was $5 a week.

"I always was an avid radio listener, so I had heard Alden on WCHV," recalled Edna Kirby Aaroe.

The voice intrigued her. She wanted to meet this fellow.

"I got to talking with a girl friend of mine who went with a boy who played in a little country band that Alden had put on the air," Edna said. "Sometimes when they were on the radio, Alden joined in and played the bass."

Edna told her girl friend: "I would love to meet Alden Aaroe."

One night Edna's telephone rang. It was her girl friend.

"I've got a blind date for you tonight," she said.

"Who with?" Edna asked.

"Alden Aaroe."

Edna was living in a boarding house near the Monticello Hotel. That night a tall, handsome, young radio announcer came to pick her up.

"He didn't have a lot of money," said Edna. "Few young people did in those days. So, on our first date we went to a public park in Charlottesville that had some animals."

The date ended in time for Alden to go back to the radio station.

"He had to read the 11 o'clock news," Edna said.

Edna Kirby, who had grown up on a small farm in nearby Yancey Mills, was then 24 years of age, three years older than Alden, and was running the lunch counter at the F.W. Woolworth's Co. store in downtown Charlottesville.

"After high school, I had gone to the National Business College in Roanoke to study to be a secretary," Edna said. "But secretarial jobs were very difficult to find, so I took a job as manager of Woolworth's lunch counter. It was one of the best places to eat lunch in downtown Charlottesville in those days."

After Edna's date with Alden, the Woolworth's lunch counter gained a new steady customer.

"Alden started coming in frequently for lunch," she said.

"He had one favorite meal. It was fried chicken, mashed potatoes, another vegetable and a glass of milk, followed by a slice of pie."

And he got all that food, Edna recalls, "for about 35 cents."

During their courtship, which lasted about two years, Alden and Edna did a lot of walking, which is an inexpensive way to date.

"The radio station was on one side of the courthouse and I lived on the other side," Edna recalled. "Alden would call and say meet me at the statue at the courthouse at 3:04, or some such precise time.

"One summer day he came by my place after a hard rain and asked me to go for a walk. We started walking toward the radio station and when we got to a low-hanging tree, Alden ran ahead of me and grabbed the tree and shook it so that I got soaked by all that rain water."

This trick was one he would play all his life.

"Always, after a rain," daughter Anna Lou said, "Daddy would say, 'Let's go for a walk. Let's go see if the rain blew anything down.' What he wanted to do was shake a wet tree when you walked under it. Dogwood trees were his favorite for that. And all of us fell for it every time."

He had been a playful trickster as a child, and now that he was a young man, he was still a playful trickster. This characteristic of his personality never would change. Throughout his life, Alden Aaroe was a guy who loved to play tricks on people.

His tricks often involved water, because he delighted in getting other people wet.

"If you walked up to him when he was watering the bushes or washing his car, you were going to get wet." Anna Lou said. "He loved to squirt people with a water hose.

"And he absolutely adored water guns, which he kept in

the refrigerator. We were all very wise never to have given him one of those new high-powered water guns because we all would have gotten soaked many times."

One favorite family story is the time Edna was taking a hot shower after working in the yard. Alden retrieved one of his water guns from the refrigerator, sneaked into the bathroom and shot Edna with stream of icy water.

"I was so mad!" Edna said. "I jumped out of the shower and chased him all around the house until I caught him and got him wet."

Anna Lou was a child at that time, but she remembers the day Mama, wearing nothing but her birthday suit, chased Daddy around the house after he had shot her with a water gun filled with ice water.

"I thought it was so funny," Anna Lou said.

Some years ago, Anna Lou asked her father what was his favorite practical joke of all time. He said it was one he had pulled on his mother years ago.

Before driving to New Jersey to pick her up to bring her to Richmond for a visit, he had called her brother, Ethan Petersen, and invited him to have lunch with them at a certain restaurant somewhere close to Philadelphia. The trick was that Alden was not going to tell his mother that her brother Ethan would be joining them for lunch.

When we pull into the parking lot at the restaurant, Alden told Ethan, I want you to be there to open the car door for her.

Ethan agreed to go along with the gag.

"So they arrived at the restaurant," Anna Lou said, "and, sure enough, Uncle Ethan was waiting right there to open the door."

Anna P. got out of the car and took a look at Ethan. Turning to Alden, she said: "That man looks just like my brother Ethan."

Like the Tar Baby, Ethan didn't say anything.

They started into the restaurant and Anna P. turned around to take another look at the man who had opened the car door for her.

"My, he really does look like my brother Ethan!" she said again.

To which a beaming Alden said: "It's because it is your brother Ethan."

Anna Lou figures the reason Alden was so proud of that trick probably was "due to the fact it was so hard to pull anything over on Anna P."

One time in their courtship days Edna and Alden were "roughing it up" in front of the boarding house where she lived in Charlottesville.

"Alden went to his car and got a rope out of the trunk," she said. "He always carried ropes in his car, until the bungee cord was invented. Then he always had bungee cords in his car instead of ropes. He thought the bungee cord was one of the greatest inventions ever."

On the day they were "roughing it up," Alden got a rope and tied Edna to a big tree. Securely. She could not get loose. Then he got into his car and drove off. Edna was furious.

"After awhile," Edna said, "he came back bringing me a treat: a 10-cent ice cream cone, which was two scoops in those days. He untied me and I ate the ice cream cone. Alden was the kind of person you could get very angry with, but you could not stay angry with him for long."

One of their favorite dates in those years was to go to the C&O train station and watch the railroaders switch engines.

"Alden loved trains," Edna said.

"We would go to the C&O station and sit for hours watching them switch those steam engines. Alden would look at the puffs of smoke and make out all sorts of images in them.

"We got to be such regular visits there that on several occasions, the engineers took us for a ride in the cabs and they let Alden drive the train up and down the track while they were turning it around."

When a second world war erupted in Europe, the lives of Alden Aaroe and Edna Kirby were about to take a turn.

"When World War II broke out," Edna said, "it became clear to everybody that United States was soon going to be at war again. So the federal government started advertising jobs for people in Washington."

Alden encouraged Edna to go to the nation's capital and apply for a job as a secretary.

"He wanted me to have the opportunity to use my secretarial skills," she said.

Edna went to Washington and applied with the Navy Department for a secretarial job, which she got. She was sworn into the Navy on Dec. 6, 1941 -- one day before the Japanese bombed Pearl Harbor.

Edna left Charlottesville and moved to Washington. But her romance with Alden Aaroe was just heating up.

Throughout December, 1941, and January, 1942, the couple got together on weekends. One weekend she went to Charlottesville. The next weekend he went to Washington.

On Saturday, Jan. 31, 1942, Alden drove to Washington to do more than just see Edna. He had a job to do for WCHV.

"Alden was doing the radio play-by-play of a boxing match and a basketball game between Virginia and the University of Maryland," Edna said.

The boxing match was in the afternoon. The basketball game was at night. Driving his little Chevrolet coupe, Alden picked up Edna in Washington and they drove out to the Maryland campus in nearby College Park.

After he had finished his broadcast of the boxing match, he and Edna went out to the car in the parking lot. And that's where Alden Aaroe asked Edna Kirby to marry him.

She said yes, and he went back into the gymnasium to broadcast the basketball game between the universities of Virginia and Maryland.

"He proposed to me in his car between the boxing match and the basketball game," Edna said.

They decided to get married right away, the following week.

But, first, Alden had something important to do. On the Monday morning after he and Edna decided to marry, he drove to Richmond to enlist in the U.S. Army Air Forces' aviation cadet program.

His interest in aviation went back to his boyhood, when his mother took him to the 1933 Chicago World's Fair, also known as Chicago's Century of Progress Exposition. There, at age 15, Alden saw an airplane up close for the first time.

On Thursday of that same week, Alden drove back to Washington to pick up Edna at her office on her lunch break. The date was Feb. 5, 1942.

He had a Maryland marriage license in hand.

"For some reason, Alden wanted to get married in Annapolis," Edna said. "So we drove to Annapolis and got married there in the home of a pastor on my lunch break."

He was three months shy of his 24th birthday. She was 26.

They had no honeymoon. Edna had to go back to work in Washington and Alden had to return to Charlottesville. The honeymoon would come later, after he had entered the Army Air Forces.

His orders came in the mail in the spring of 1942. He caught a train to Richmond, where he caught a train to Amarillo, Tex., for basic training.

"As I remember," Edna said, "Alden had 25 cents in his pocket and a bag of oranges. He ate oranges all the way to Amarillo."

He finished basic training in June and was sent to a military base in East St. Louis, Ill., just across the Mississippi River from St. Louis. There, four months after their wedding in Annapolis, Alden and Edna Aaroe had their honeymoon.

"I caught the train one weekend to St. Louis," Edna said. "You know how hot St. Louis can be in the summer. Well, when I got off the train, the temperature was at least 100 degrees.

"We got a room in an air-conditioned hotel. Alden had gotten his first Army paycheck, so he said we were going to celebrate by getting a room in a big hotel with air-conditioning."

His next assignment was Enid, Okla., and by this time, the young newlyweds were ready to spend some time together.

After all, they both knew that Alden, like thousands and thousands of young men, soon would be going off to war.

Late in the summer of 1942, Edna quit her secretarial job with the Navy Department in Washington and caught a train to Oklahoma to join Alden.

"The train was full of soldiers in uniform and other wives going to meet their husbands," Edna said. "All of us were so excited and keyed up. We stayed up all night talking about our lives."

Even though Edna and Alden were reunited in Enid, they could not live together. Married cadets in the program had to live in barracks on the base, and their wives had to find housing off the base.

Rooms in private homes were plentiful.

"Everybody knew the situation and people were very kind to us," Edna said. "Many of the people had sons who had gone off to war, so they knew what we were going through. They went out of their way to accomodate us."

Edna and the wife of another cadet shared a room in a home.

When his training program in Enid was completed in Janury of 1943, Alden was commissioned a second lieutenant and sent to Lubbock, Tex., where he learned to fly large transport planes.

"Alden was too tall to fly a fighter plane or a bomber," Edna said. "In fact, he barely got into the Air Forces because of his height. So that's why he had to fly cargo planes."

Edna followed him to Lubbock, where they finally got to live togeher.

They went in with another couple and shared a two-bedroom apartment in a fraternity house on the campus of Texas Tech University. College campuses had plenty of housing available because so many students had joined the military.

"The fraternity house was very close to the base, and the boys could come home every night," Edna said.

Some college boys were living in the fraternity house, and

the first day they noticed these two young women hanging around, they started flirting.

"Oh, they were giving us a hard time," Edna said. "But when they saw those two big soldiers in uniform coming in the house that evening, that stopped the flirting right there."

Alden got his wings in Lubbock.

"That was a big event," Edna said. "He was so proud of getting those wings. And I was proud of him, too."

From Lubbock, Alden was sent to Austin, Tex., for a month.

He and Edna rented a small apartment in Austin.

"The bathroom was so tiny that Alden always bumped his head on the ceiling when he got out of the bathtub," she said.

The young pilot's next assignment was a base in the Southern California desert. Once again, he and Edna boarded a train and headed for yet another new place to call home for a short while.

"We couldn't ride in the same coach because Alden had to ride with other soldiers," Edna recalled. "He was 23 cars behind me. He got in a gin rummy game and won about $20. So he walked through 23 cars to bring the money to me. He was afraid if he kept it he would spend it or lose it."

In the desert, Alden practiced night flying.

"They would go up at night and drop paratroopers," Edna said.

After about one month in the California desert, they caught a train to Fort Sumner, New Mexico, where they lived for three months in a rented room in an adobe house owned by a Mexican woman who spoke Spanish.

"That house had walls 18 inches thick," Edna recalled.

By now, it was the summer of 1943 and Alden Aaroe had been training for about a year at seven different military bases.

He still did not know where he would be sent in the war.

His next assignment was a base near Laurinburg, N.C. Alden flew across country. Edna rode in the car of another pilot's wife. They were scheduled to stay in Laurinburg just two weeks, so they rented a hotel room.

"We had to show our marriage certificate to the desk before he would rent us the room," Edna said.

Next came the moment Alden had been waiting for: His overseas orders.

"Alden had to go to Fort Wayne in Indiana for his orders," Edna said.

"So he and the other boys flew to Fort Wayne, and I went there in a car with the same girl I had ridden with from New Mexico."

The overseas orders were handed out in a large room. The pilots were called out of the room to be handed their orders, which were sealed, and an officer's sidearm.

"When they came back into the room, they had their orders in hand and a gun in a holster strapped to them," Edna said. "They were all excited and whooping it up, and, of course, all of us wives were in tears."

Alden and the other pilots were all pumped up.

"They were like kids at Christmas," Edna said.

The sealed orders were not to be opened until the pilots got to Miami, their jumping-off point. When Alden opened his orders, he learned he had been assigned to Cairo, Egypt, the headquarters of the U.S. armed forces in the Middle East.

In the summer of 1943, Alden took off for ancient Egypt. Edna, now pregnant, headed back to Charlottesville. She rented an apartment on Jefferson Park Avenue and stayed there until he came home from the war.

Three months after he arrived in Cairo, Alden was transferred to Teheran, Iran, headquarters of the Persian Gulf Command.

Iran, an ancient land once known as Persia, had declared neutrality in 1939 when World War II broke out in Europe with Germany's invasion of Poland. But the Allies coveted Iran's strategic location. They wanted to use the Trans-Iranian railroad to move supplies from England to the Soviet Union. When Iran's ruler, Reza Shah, refused to let the Allies use the railway in 1941, British and Soviet troops invaded Iran. Reza Shah was replaced by his son, Mohammad Reza Pahlavia, who signed a treaty letting the Allies use the rail line.

Futhermore, the Allies were allowed to establish military bases in Iran. Two American bases were established in Iran's capital, Teheran, and it was at one of those bases that Lt. Alden Aaroe was stationed from the fall of 1943 until the war ended in 1945.

One family photograph shows Alden standing beside his transport plane at the base in Teheran. Written on the plane's nose is the name Alden gave it: "Edna Kay." He had named it for his wife in Charlottesville.

During his two years in Iran, Aaroe was promoted to the rank of captain and amassed an estimated 2,000 flying hours in which he piloted transport planes delivering supplies, materials and paratroopers on support missions to many destinations, including the Middle East, the Soviet Union and over the hump to India.

He was fortunate in that he had no accidents. But he did have some close calls. One night, while attempting to land in Khartoum, the capital of Sudan, only half of the landing lights were turned on and Aaroe's plane nearly ended up in the Nile River.

Aaroe loved aviation, although he never showed any serious interest in flying airplanes after the war. In his later years, he wrote a brief note describing flight. The note read as follows:

"Aviation of itself is not inheriently dangerous; but to an even greater extent than the sea, is unremittingly unforgiving of carelessness."

Even so, Aaroe by his own admission was guilty of some careless manuevers during his days as an American flyboy. He confessed to having flown a plane under a bridge over the Mississippi near St. Louis, and to having buzzed some feluc- cas (Mediterranean sailing ships) in the Red Sea and causing them to blow over.

War failed to take the prankster out of him.

Aaroe even pulled a prank on the Shah of Iran while he was in Teheran. The Shah insisted on parking his personal

Voice of the Morning

27

locomotive at the U.S. air base, despite repeated requests by American brass to park it elsewhere. One night Aaroe recruited some of his friends and they chiseled the bronze seal off the front of the Shah's locomotive. Aaroe brought the souvenir home from the war and mounted it over his fireplace.

His daughter Anna Lou's favorite war story about her father is not one about war, but one about a bear.

"Daddy told us that when he was in Teheran, the Russians sent the Shah of Iran a Russian bear," Anna Lou said. "But the Shah did not want this bear, so somehow Daddy wound up in charge of this Russian bear."

He kept the bear in the barracks. The animal slept in a clothes hamper.

"The bear loved to ride in Daddy's Jeep," Anna Lou continued, "so Daddy would put the bear in his Jeep and drive him around the base. They always wound up at the PX, and Daddy would buy the bear an ice cream cone.

"The ice cream would melt and dribble down the bear's chest, so the bear would take his paw and scrape the melted ice cream off his chest and lick it off his paw."

Alden Aaroe and a Russian bear riding around in a Jeep! What a scene that would make in a Hollywood movie!

It was in Teheran that Alden became friends with a U.S. Army sergeant named Louis Yurachek, who was from Highland Springs, a Richmond suburb.

Through that friendship, Alden met a wealthy Teheran doctor, whose last name was Gharagglou, and his American wife, Catherine.

Living with Dr. and Mrs. Gharagglou and their two daughters, Mary and Tutty, was a young Irani girl named Muty Zandi, whose parents worked as domestic servants for the family.

Muty, who had been born in a rural area in Iran, often accompanied the Gharagglou daughters to Red Cross-sponsored dances for servicemen stationed in Teheran, and at one of those dances she met Louis Yurachek.

Eventually, they married and Louis brought his young Irani wife home to Richmond, where they settled and raised a family, and where Muty's name was Americanized to Judy.

Louis died in 1992, but Judy Yurachek still lives in their home in the Henrico County suburbs of Richmond.

She remembers the war years in Teheran very well.

When she and Louis Yurachek met at the Red Cross dance, it was love at first sight for him.

"But not for me!" Judy Yuracheck recalled with a laugh.

After they met, Louis started making regular visits to the Gharagglous' large home in Teheran. He usually was accompanied by his friend, Alden Aaroe.

"Louis and Alden came to the house a lot when they were off-duty," Mrs. Yurachek said. "The house had a large library with a lot of books, and they liked to sit in the library and read."

Alden made a good impression on the Gharagglou family.

"Everybody liked him a lot," Mrs. Yurachek said. "He had a wonderful sense of humor and was so nice and kind to all of us."

She remembers one Christmas Day in Teheran when a man dressed like Santa Claus showed up at the house.

"This man in a red suit and with a big belly came very early one Christmas morning with chocolates and chewing gum for me, Mary and Tutty," Mrs. Yurachek. "We had never seen a Santa Claus and so we were very excited."

The Santa Claus was Alden Aaroe.

Smitten by the pretty Irani girl, Louis Yurachek asked her to marry him.

"At first I said no way," Judy Yurachek said. "I didn't want to marry anybody. I was so young. Besides, my mother was very upset by this."

Louis kept asking and Muty kept refusing.

"Sometimes I would say yes, but then I would change my mind and say no again," she said.

Finally, near the end of the war, she agreed.

"I told him, okay, I will marry you."

Although Muty Zandi was willing to marry this American soldier, it was no done deal because Louis Yurachek was having trouble getting the green light from his commanding officer.

Edna Aaroe recalls that Alden told her after the war that the Army brass was adamant about not letting Louis marry the young Irani girl.

"Since Alden was a commissioned officer, he could go to bat for Louis, which he did," Edna said.

Eventually, everything worked out and Louis and Muty were married Dec. 13, 1945, in a Catholic church in Teheran.

"We had a big church wedding, which Catherine (Gharagglou) paid for," Judy Yurachek said.

Alden was not at the wedding. The war was over and he had gone home.

When Louis and Judy Yurachek came to Richmond to build a life after the war, she was pleasantly surprised the first time she heard a familiar voice on the radio. It was the voice of the young American pilot who had been the first Santa Claus she had ever seen.

It was Richmond's voice of the morning, Alden Aaroe.

As the years flew by, Louis and Judy Yurachek often socialized with Alden Aaroe. But Alden never called her Judy.

"He said when he met me in Teheran my name was Muty and I would always be Muty to him," she said.

Chapter Three

In January, 1944, shortly after Lt. Alden Aaroe reported for duty in Teheran, Edna Kirby Aaroe gave birth to a daughter at Martha Jefferson Hospital in Charlottesville.

The baby was named Anna Louise -- Anna after Alden's mother, and Louise after Edna's middle name.

She would be called Anna Lou.

"I immediately sent Alden a cablegram with the news," Edna said, "but Anna Lou was 10 days old when he finally got the word from a man from Richmond who was an American Red Cross worker in Teheran."

In the summer of 1945, near the end of the war, American officials in Teheran gave the Shah of Iran a bomber airplane, a B-17. Alden Aaroe and a crew of aviators were assigned the job of flying the plane back to the United States to be refurbished.

As Alden told Edna the story, when they landed the plane in Rome for refueling, the lights came on in Rome for the first time since the nightly blackouts had taken effect.

Japan had surrendered and the war was over. It was August, 1945.

Alden and his crew continued their flight and landed in New York.

"Because the war was over, he did not have to go back overseas," Edna said.

Alden's first stop back in the States was his mother's apartment in Summit, N.J., where Anna P. was still teaching sixth grade.

"He went to see his mother, then he caught the train from New York to Charlottesville," Edna said.

Capt. Alden Aaroe showed up at his wife's apartment in Charlottesville wearing a new dress uniform. But he did not look good.

"His was very thin and very yellow," Edna said.

"His color was bad because he had had malaria. He was thin because he had had dysentery."

Anna Lou was 18 months old when this strange-looking man in a uniform showed up at her doorstep.

"I had been showing her pictures of Alden in his uniform in hopes she would recognize him," Edna recalled. "So when he walked up to her, she said, 'Hi, Daddy!' But since Alden didn't look at all like his pictures, I think she would have said hi-daddy to any Joe Blow in a uniform."

At first, father and daughter did not get along very well.

"Anna Lou had not seen many young men up to that point in her life, because so many of them had gone off to the war," Edna said.

"So when this young man came into her house to live, she was not very happy about it. And Alden wasn't sure what to make of her."

Anna Lou, of course, only knows what her mother has told her about her reluctance to accept her father when he came home from the war.

"Mom says that since I had been the center of her attention since the day I was born, I became very quiet and shy when, suddenly, this large man appeared in my life," Anna Lou said.

"He thought I should be able to say all my ABC's and know all my nursery rhymes, so he apparently wasn't real impressed with me, either."

The bonding took awhile, but when they bonded, it was strong.

"It took them awhile to get used to each other," Edna said. "But when they finally accepted each other, well, then, they became big buddies. She really loved her daddy and, as my friends from Georgia used to say, she was his eyeballs, which was their way of saying she was the apple of his eye."

Each year for the first twenty-one years of Anna Lou's life, her father gave her roses on her birthday -- one for each year.

"He gave me one white rose for each year for the first twelve years," she said. "On my thirteenth birthday, he gave me thirteen pink roses. I got pink roses until I turned eighteen, when he gave me eighteen red roses."

On her twenty-second birthday, the roses stopped.

"I suppose that was his way of telling me I no longer was his little girl," she said. "And, besides, by that time roses were getting pretty expensive, and Daddy always watched his money very closely!"

Anna Lou's earliest memories of her father go back to when she was three or four years old.

"I mainly remember him being playful and a lot of fun," she said.

"He read me fairy tales a lot, and one of his favorite things to do was change the endings of the fairy tales. When Daddy read them, the wolf ate the three little pigs, and the fox ate Henny Penny. All of which made me livid. I would shout: 'NO! NO! NO! THAT'S NOT THE WAY IT'S SUPPOSED TO BE, DADDY!' "

But all the time she was thinking how funny her daddy was.

As Anna Lou remembers it, the first time she ever heard Alden's voice on the radio was one night when the whole family was having dinner and listening to the radio. She was very young at the time.

"All of a sudden Daddy's voice comes out of the radio," she said. "Now, I knew my father worked for the radio station, but I did not know about how his voice could be pre-recorded."

She looked at the radio. Then she looked at Alden across from her at the dining table and said: "I have TWO daddies!"

Alden called her "Baby Bear" and her nickname for him was "Poppa Bear."

"He was very much the Poppa Bear type," Anna Lou said. "He was large. He could growl and be gruff. He had these big paws. So I always called him Poppa Bear and my children always called him Poppa Bear, too."

When Anna Lou became an adult, the personal letters she received from her father often were signed "Pbearaaroe."

The nickname was appropriate for another reason.

"Poppa Bear definitely was the head of the clan," Anna Lou said. "There was never any question in the household about who was in charge. And so as a little girl I was very careful to do what Poppa Bear said so I would make Poppa

Bear happy."

Alden had been home from the war only a short while when he suffered a recurrence of malaria. He was so sick with fever that he had to be hospitalized at an Army hospital at Fort Dix in New Jersey.

"He had bouts with malaria for several years after the war," Edna said. "He would get chills and shake all over."

Aaroe remained on active duty with the Army Air Forces for several months after the war ended. Near the end of 1945, he was mustered out.

He did remain in the Reserves, however, for a number of years on a non-flying status, and eventually was promoted to major.

Out of the service, Alden took back his job as an announcer with radio station WCHV in Charlottesville.

"His salary was very low, especially in light of the fact that in Iran he had been getting a captain's pay, plus per diem, plus flight pay," Edna said. "As I recalled, his pay in the Army had been something like $600 a month, and I think the radio station gave him around $100 a month."

Since he was now a man with a family, Alden was discouraged.

He started shopping around for other jobs. He applied to be a commercial pilot for TWA and he applied for broadcasting jobs with radio stations in New York and Richmond.

In an interview on his 40th anniversary at Richmond's WRVA, Aaroe told a newspaper reporter how he landed in Richmond in 1946.

He said: "In those days, commercial pilots worked every weekend, and I didn't want to do that because I had a young daughter at home whom I barely knew because of the war. And I didn't really want to go to New York because I had fallen in love with Virginia during my student days at the University of Virginia. And Richmond, being the state's capital, seemed like an important place to be in the radio business. I wanted to be part of that."

And so he came to Richmond for a job interview with

WRVA, the city's first radio station and its most influential.

"Alden drove to Richmond on his own," Edna Aaroe said. "They auditioned him, and he went back a second time before he got the job."

He got the job because John Tansey was very high on him.

Tansey was a Miami native with a journalism degree from the University of Florida who had worked briefly at the university's radio station (WRUF) in Gainesville after graduating in 1940. He had landed an announcing job at WRVA in the fall of 1940, arriving in Richmond with a couple of suitcases and the clothes on his back.

After the Japanese bombed Pearl Harbor in December of 1941, Tansey joined the U. S. Navy's officer training program. He spent most of the war at sea, serving on ships all over the world, from the Arctic Circle to the Persian Gulf to the South Pacific.

When the war ended, Tansey returned to WRVA and soon was promoted to production manager. That was the job he was holding when Alden Aaroe showed up for a job interview.

"I was very impressed with Alden," Tansey recalled. "I wanted to hire the guy on the spot."

But there was a salary disagreement, Tansey recalled with a smile.

"Alden wanted something like $250 a month and we were offering something like $225 a month," Tansey said.

Tansey went to bat for Aaroe.

"I finally cajoled management into hiring him at an extra $25 or so a month, and I suppose you could say we got our money's worth," said Tansey, who is fond of calling Aaroe his "most famous hire."

On the first day of February in 1946, Alden Aaroe, then 27 years old, reported for work as a staff announcer at the WRVA studios in the old Hotel Richmond in downtown Richmond at the corner of East Grace and 9th streets.

Across 9th Street stood Mr. Jefferson's Capitol.

Across Grace Street stood St. Paul's Episcopal Church,

where Robert E. Lee had worshiped from time to time during the American Civil War.

Forty-seven years after his first day on the job in the Hotel Richmond, Aaroe's funeral service would be held across the street in the church where Lee had prayed.

Family lore has it that when Alden took the job, he and Edna had $17 in their bank account.

"They may not have been that broke," Tansey said, "but they were struggling. Alden started from scratch and lived in a very humble manner for years."

When he came to Richmond, Alden had to find a place for his family to live.

"He hunted for days," Edna said. "He finally rented a small guest house behind a large, three-story house that had been built in the 1800s."

This guest house connected to a large house by a breezeway was in Henrico County on the west side of Richmond on what was then Ridge Road, but what today is Parham Road. Both structures are gone. Where they stood is the site of Colonial Place Christian Church, 1200 Parham Road.

Alden moved into the rental house first while Edna and Anna Lou remained in Charlottesville. Two months later, on April Fool's Day in 1946, Edna and Anna Lou moved in with him.

"After I spent a week cleaning it," Edna recalled.

Alden's and Edna's first home in Richmond was no palace. It had two rooms and a bath. His buddies at worked dubbed it the "Chicken House."

They lived in the little rental house for about two years.

One weekend while they were living there, Alden went to New Jersey to visit his mother in Summit. He drove the little Chevy coupe, the same car in which he had asked Edna to marry him, to Washington, where he parked the car in a garage and continued the trip by train.

"When Alden got back to Washington Sunday evening," Edna said, "his car was gone. It had been stolen out of the garage."

He was scheduled to be at work Monday morning at the crack of dawn to read the news and give the farm report, so he caught a bus to Richmond.

"He got home very late," Edna said. "Then he got up at three in the morning and set out on foot to the nearest bus stop, which was at the corner of Patterson Avenue and Three Chopt Road, to catch a city bus downtown to get to work on time."

The story does not surprise John Tansey.

"I don't think Alden ever missed a day of work," Tansey said. "I was telling him this at his 75th birthday party and he said, 'Well, I may have missed one or two days.' But I don't remember him ever missing a day. He was Mr. Dependability."

Anna Lou remembers that her father did call in sick occasionally, whenever a bad cold caused him to lose his voice.

"We were always glad it did not happen often," Anna Lou said. "Daddy was a terrible patient."

For three weeks after his car was stolen in Washington, he followed the same go-to-work routine. He got up in the middle of the night and walked approximately two miles to the bus stop to catch the bus downtown.

"We didn't know anybody who would lend us a car," Edna said. "And we lived too far out to ask any of his colleagues at the radio station to come pick him up. And we didn't have enough money to buy another car."

At the end of three weeks, the telephone rang.

It was the police department in Baltimore.

"The Baltimore police had found his car," Edna said. "The thieves had driven it to Baltimore and abandoned it there."

Alden caught a bus to Baltimore to pick up his little Chevy, which was in fine shape.

"The thieves had not hurt it whatsoever," Edna said.

In fact, they had improved the vehicle by installing a radio in the dash. Furthermore, they had left a nice quilt on the back seat.

"By having his car stolen," Edna said, "Alden gained a car

radio and a quilt."

Their closest neighbors out there at the Chicken House had a goat that everybody called Heathcliff. Whenever Edna hung out the wash to dry on the clothesline, the goat made a habit of eating the buttons off Alden's shirts.

On many weekends during the two years Alden and Edna lived in the small rental house, staff members from WRVA would go out there with their wives and dates to socialize.

"We used to go out there to the Chicken House on Sunday afternoons to play volleyball and have a picnic," John Tansey said. "None of us had any money, so that was pretty much the only recreation we could afford. We always had a lot of fun."

One popular activity on those Sundays was to take a walk through the woods just beyond the city limits of Richmond.

"That was considered way out in the country in those days," John Tansey said. "There were a lot of woods to walk in, so we did a lot of walking and a lot of exploring the territory.

"One time when we were walking we found an old farmer who lived out there off a rutted road. We started walking over to his place a lot to visit him, and he and Alden became close friends."

The farmer's last name was Gilbert, and their friendship led to a business deal. Aaroe, looking for a place to build a home, bought a piece of the man's property, part of which included the highest point in Henrico County.

What Aaroe purchased was a wooded, three-acre lot. It was located off Ridge Road, not too far from where Grove Avenue Baptist Church later was built, and very close to the intersection of Patterson Avenue and Parham Road, both of which were two-lane country roads in the late 1940s.

On that lot Alden and Edna Aaroe built their first home -- literally.

"Alden drew the plans and he built it almost entirely with his own hands, although I helped with the work, too," Edna Aaroe said.

Alden's plans called for constructing a small house with

two rooms, a bathroom and a kitchen. Small was all the young couple could afford.

"After we bought the land from Mr. Gilbert," Edna said, "we had used all the money we had saved during the war. So we were sort of broke."

They started squirreling away money again. Soon they had enough to start buying materials.

"Material was very hard to get, especially lumber," Edna said. "But my sister's husband, who was just back from the war, too, had a lumber company in Harrisonburg, and he arranged for us to buy some lumber.

"We rented a truck and drove to Harrisonburg and picked up a load of lumber. All the rafters. The two-by-fours. What have you. The wood had been kiln-dried and it was the toughest wood to drive a nail in that you can imagine. John Tansey will confirm that."

Tansey did confirm that.

"That wood Alden built his first house with was so hard, it was almost impossible to drive a nail in it," Tansey said.

Tansey was among Alden's WRVA colleagues who pitched in to help the Aaroes with their ambitious house-building project that required countless hours and a painful dose of back-straining labor.

"A lot of us from the station went out there in our spare time to help," Tansey said. "I remember that one of our engineers helped him with the electrical wiring."

Before they could start building their first home, numerous trees had to be cut down.

"The lot was nothing but trees," Edna said. "So the first thing Alden did was cut down a lot of trees so we could have a driveway leading out to Ridge Road. And then he had to cut down a lot of trees to clear a spot where we wanted to build the house. And, of course, he had pull the stumps out of the ground, which he did using his ropes and his car."

The tree-cutting project was right down Aaroe's alley.

"Alden loved to cut down trees," Edna said. "And he was very good at it. He could fell a 60-foot tree exactly where he wanted it to fall."

Watching it fall and yelling "TIMBER!" became a family tradition, Anna Lou recalls. And once a tree was on the ground, she would walk on its trunk while Alden sawed off the branches.

Alden also loved to chop wood. Whenever he wanted to get something off his mind, he'd go outside and split firewood. The Aaroes always had a big stack of firewood and kindling beside the house.

Whenever Alden's daughter, Anna Lou, smells wood, she thinks of her father.

"I associate a smell with Daddy, and that is the smell of wood and wood shavings," she said. "He always was either cutting down a tree, pulling up the stump of a tree, splitting logs to burn in the fireplace, or building something made of wood. He absolutely loved wood."

It took them nine months to build the "Little House," as it came to be known affectionately.

"Alden would go to work in the morning and do what he had to do, and I would get all my chores done at the Chicken House, where we lived the whole time we were building the Little House," Edna said.

"When he came home in the afternoon, we packed up our things and took them over to the Little House to work on it."

Anna Lou, by now three years old, always was with them during these long work sessions.

"Alden bought a huge wheelbarrow, and while we were working, we put a blanket in the wheelbarrow and Anna Lou took her afternoon naps in it," Edna said. "That child could sleep anywhere!"

Several years ago, Alden gave his daughter the wheelbarrow in which she took afternoon naps during the construction of the Little House.

"Daddy was a master of peculiar gifts, especially at Christmas," Anna Lou said. "He loved to give you old family things at Christmas. One year he gave me the hat his great-grandmother wore coming over on the boat from

Denmark."

Although Anna Lou took naps in the wheelbarrow, she didn't sleep through the entire house-building project. No, indeed. Her mother will tell you she was a curious child who got into things.

"When we were building the foundation of the Little House," Edna recalled, "we had to use a trowel, of course, to put the mortar between the cinder blocks. Anna Lou would pick up a trowel to play with it, and the next thing you knew, Alden was asking, 'Where's my trowel?'

"Well, it was always down the hole of a cinder block, right where Anna Lou had dropped it. There must be six or seven trowels in the foundation of the Little House."

There were no water pipes on their property, so they had to dig a well. Eventually, they had to dig a second well. The land on which the first one was dug was taken by the county to put up a water tower, a piece of government meddling that had Alden all revved up for awhile.

At long last, Alden and Edna finished building their house in the woods, and in the summer of 1948, they packed up their belongings in the Chicken House and moved into their beloved Little House, which they had built with their own blood, sweat and tears.

"We were just delighted to finally be moving into our own house," Edna said.

Not long after they moved into the Little House, Edna Aaroe discovered she was pregnant. They decided to add a third room, which would serve as the living room, thus allowing the original two rooms to be bedrooms.

"Alden hired somebody to build the living room," Edna said. "It was a very nice room with pine-panelled walls, a high ceiling and a fireplace."

They also added a garage, which Alden needed not to park automobiles, but to store all his tools and to use as a workshop.

"No cars ever lived in an Alden Aaroe garage," Anna Lou said. "The garage was where he kept his ever-growing collection of tools, lawn equipment and tractors."

The third room got built, but the second baby never came.

"I had a miscarriage," Edna said. "Later on I had two more miscarriages. We wanted more children, but it was not to be.

"With Anna Lou, however, we got a wonderful child. She was a jewel, just a perfect baby. We took her everywhere we went and she behaved beautifully. I don't remember her ever having a temper tantrum."

Chapter Four

When they moved into the Little House, there was no neighborhood around them.

"We literally were living in the woods," Edna Aaroe said. "When it got dark at night, it really got dark."

Anna Lou had no neighborhood children to play with.

"We were really by ourselves out there," Anna Lou said. "There just weren't any playmates for me close by, which is why I remember all the pets we had so well."

Realizing that their child needed to have some interaction with other children for social reasons, Alden and Edna enrolled Anna Lou in a nursery school program when she was four years old.

"We put Anna Lou in nursery school at Trinity Methodist Church on Forest Avenue so she would get used to playing with other children," Edna said.

This decision brought chickens into their lives.

"One day at nursery school," Edna recalled, "the children went to a chicken farm, where each of the children was given a baby chick to take home. Anna Lou came home with one little peeper. We put it in a box by the stove and it peeped all night long and kept us awake."

Alden figured the chick was lonely for other chicks, so the next morning he told Edna: "Go to Southern States today and buy two more baby chickens to go with that chicken."

Now they owned chickens.

"We really got interested in keeping chickens," Edna said. "So Alden built a chicken house out in the back yard."

In the heyday of their chicken-raising years, they usually had 16 hens and one rooster.

"So we had all the fresh eggs you'd ever want," Edna said. "We had so many eggs we even sold them to different people."

Having chickens around the house made Edna feel right at home. After all, when she was a girl growing up on her family's farm in Yancey Mills, they always had chickens.

"Every year right after Christmas," Edna said, "my mother used to order her baby chicks from Rhode Island -- the famous Rhode Island Reds. We had to keep watch at the

Yancey Mills post office every day until sometime in March when my mother's little peepers arrived.

"They came in by train in a cardboard box, then the people at the train station would take them to the post office because we did not have rural delivery at that time."

Edna's mother tended to the chickens. She fed them and collected the eggs. But Edna got the job of killing the chickens when it was time to throw one in the pot.

"When the chickens got any size, my mother would grade them and then we'd kill all the roosters but one," Edna recalled. "That was my job as a girl, because I really was a tomboy. I killed the chickens on Saturday and got them plucked and cut up and dressed, so they were ready to be cooked for dinner on Sunday."

After Alden and Edna started raising chickens beside the Little House, they decided to order some Rhode Island Reds, the same breed of chicken Edna's family always raised back in Yancey Mills.

When their order came in, it included hens and roosters.

"I killed all the roosters but one," Edna said.

They named this chosen rooster Bill.

"Bill was a great big rooster with the greatest comb you've ever seen, and the loudest crow at the crack of dawn you've ever heard," Edna said. "Thank goodness we didn't have any neighbors, because we sure would have heard a lot of complaints about Bill.

One afternoon Alden and Edna were working in their garden when they decided to take a break inside the house. Alden set Anna Lou on a tree stump beside the garden, handed her a big stick and told her to keep the chickens out of the garden.

"We used to turn them out of the chicken house late in the afternoon so they could walk around the yard and scratch," Edna said.

Anna Lou was four or five years old at that time.

"At that age," she said, "a rooster looks like a very big creature. I remember sitting there on the stump and looking at Bill, and thinking, 'I don't like this.'"

Soon after Alden and Edna went into the house, Bill the rooster got into the tomatoes.

"So Anna Lou took off after him with the stick," Edna said. "And when she did, Bill turned and started running right at her. She got scared and started running toward the house, at which time she tripped over the root of a tree stump and fell down."

Bill the rooster seized the moment.

"He jumped on her and started pecking her on the head," Edna said. "And, of course, she started shrieking. Alden ran out of the house as fast as he could go and got the rooster off Anna Lou."

Tears streaming down her face, Anna Lou got up, ran to her mother's arms and screeched: "Put him in the pot! Put him in the pot!"

One Sunday not long after that, Edna served a particularly tough chicken for dinner. When they finished eating, Edna confessed: "Well, we just ate Bill the rooster."

Alden and Anna Lou broke down in tears.

Once a neighborhood grew up around them, they got rid of their chickens. An assortment of other animals, however, always were a constant part of family life. Dogs. Cats. Rabbits. One time, they briefly kept a donkey with a Biblical name: Nicodemus. The donkey was a fixture on the WRVA-sponsored Old Dominion Barn Dance, which Aaroe emceed in those days.

Nicodemus did not live with them for long, but there are family pictures of the donkey.

"Daddy loved animals," Anna Lou said. "Any kind of animals.

"Our first dog was a female Belgian shepherd. To be more accurate, mostly Belgian shepherd. Pedigree was not important in our dogs. We named her Shep, but we almost always called her Sheppy."

Alden built a pen in the yard to keep Sheppy from getting loose.

But dogs have a way of escaping pens.

"One weekend when we had gone up to the country, Sheppy got out of her pen," Edna Aaroe recalled. "She was gone when we got home and she stayed gone for several days until she finally came home, all worn out."

Not long after she came home exhausted from her wandering, Sheppy gave birth to a litter of pups. No surprise there, given the inclinations of dogs on the prowl.

"One morning I saw Sheppy come out of a big pile of lumber in the yard," Edna said. "I suspected something was up, so I went out to the lumber pile and found nine brand-new puppies in there.

"Alden had already gone to work, so I called him at the station to tell him he had become the father of nine puppies overnight. He was thrilled to death, so as soon as he came up he started building a great big doghouse."

The doghouse was just one of the countless things Aaroe built in the course of his life, for he was a man who loved to build things with his hands.

"Daddy believed that what men do is build things," Anna Lou said. "I suppose he learned that from his grandfather on the farm in New Jersey.

"He had a knack for it, but he was not a fine craftsman. The best thing you can say about anything Daddy built is that it was sturdy. It was built to survive earthquake, tornado and flood.

"If he were in doubt, he used two-by-fours. And his plywood always was at least three-quarters of an inch thick, or, more likely an inch thick. Things he built were never flimsy. They were thick. You might not be able to pick it up and move it, but it was not going to break."

Sheppy and her puppies went to live in Alden's great big doghouse, and Anna Lou remembers spending day after day with her head stuck in the doghouse door, playing with the puppies and making sure they were all right.

After awhile they decided to keep one of the puppies and

give the other eight away, which Alden did by offering them to his listeners.

"He had 50,000 watts to help him get rid of those dogs," Edna said.

The one puppy they kept also was called Sheppy, or Sheppy Two as long as the first Sheppy was still alive. Alden and the second Sheppy, a male, got along famously. When he died in 1961, Alden wrapped his body in the leather pilot's jacket from the war, and buried him out in the yard beneath a dogwood tree.

One listener who took one of the first Sheppy's litter was a Powhatan County woman named Mattie Balmer, who took a female pup named Pat.

Not long after giving the pups away, Aaroe was driving back to Richmond one night after one of his many public appearances. Edna and Anna Lou were with him. Passing through Powhatan County, he pulled off the main highway and drove to a farm house.

Alden got out of the car and yelled at the house: "Mattie! You know who this is?"

A woman came hustling out of the house and shouted: "Lord, it's Alden Aaroe!"

A friendship was born.

"We visited Mrs. Balmer many times, probably once a month for years," Anna Lou said. "We'd go out there to the country to see the cows and ride the tractor and take long walks. Daddy really loved visiting that farm and the neighboring farm. I'm sure it took him back to his childhood days on his grandparents' farm in New Jersey."

The neighboring farm on Cosby Road in Powhatan was the home of Maude Cosby, Mattie Baumer's sister. Another house nearby was the home of Robert and Dorothy Cosby. Robert was the nephew of Maude and Mattie.

Dorothy Cosby, who still lives in the same place across the field from Mattie Balmer's house, remembers well those days when Alden Aaroe and his wife, Miss Edna, and his daughter, Anna Lou, came visiting.

"Lord, they used to come out here all the time!" said Mrs. Cosby, a retired Powhatan County schoolteacher. "And we always had such a grand time."

Whenever Alden planned to visit Mrs. Balmer and the Cosbys, he always announced it on the radio, according to Dorothy Cosby.

"He'd say, 'I'm closing up shop early so I can get on out to Powhatan to visit Uncle Joe today,'" Mrs. Cosby recalled.

"When we heard that we'd all get ready for him. We'd get out the hams and start baking cakes and cooking food, because Alden loved to eat."

During one visit on a wintry day when snow was in the forecast, Dorothy Cosby, who was still teaching at that time, told Alden she wished schools would be closed the next day so she could say home and bake a cake for her husband.

Lo and behold, the next morning it was snowing and the superintendent of schools in Powhatan closed the schools.

"At six o'clock that morning," Mrs. Cosby said, "I was in my kitchen making breakfast and listening to Alden on the radio. Suddenly he said, 'Dorothy, you can bake Robert's cake today, because the schools in Powhatan are closed.' Well, it startled me so much I dropped an egg on the floor!"

Dorothy Cosby remembers one Sunday afternoon when two people on motorcycles pulled up in front of Mattie Balmer's house.

"Alden was riding one motorcycle and Miss Edna was riding the other," Mrs. Cosby said.

Aaroe's fling with motorcycles began in the fall of 1964 when he invested in a business deal with the Honda House motorcycle dealership. To promote the product, he kept a Honda motorcycle at home and frequently rode it.

In those days he was teaching Sunday school at River Road Baptist Church, and on Sunday mornings, weather permitting, he often rode to church on his motorcycle wearing his Sunday suit, a hat on his head, his pipe sticking out of his mouth, and his Bible tied to the cycle's rack with a bungee cord.

He later gave up riding a motorcycle, but after one oil crisis in the 1970s drove gasoline prices skyhigh, Aaroe went out and bought a motorcycle.

"Just in case we have another oil crisis," he told family and friends.

Alden shared the news of his 1964 venture with Honda House in a letter to Anna Lou, who at the time was living in Farmville, Va., with her first husband, Stan Willett, then a pre-med student at Hampden-Sydney College.

Aaroe wrote to his daughter:

"I always suffer a bit from indecision when I am about to invest or speculate as ever you consider it. I get jumpy. I seek shelter in the nearest sand pile, and such a day was yesterday. I signed the dotted line committing myself, time and money into the Honda venture... I had to retreat to the woodpile and drive the axe time and time again into the sinews of the wood to be able to clear my head of fears, apprehensions, doubts, and all the little ogres that beset me. But as time moved on and I grew tired and a little spent, a realization of the fact that it was a venture, that I was not alone, that there are odds in my favor, and soon I settled down with Pearl Buck in the big chair and relaxed."

Financial matters always fretted Alden Aaroe, a child of the Great Depression in the 1930s.

"Daddy grew up in the Depression and he was always ready in case it ever came back," Anna Lou said. "One of his favorite sayings was there's no such thing as a free lunch. He was not a gloom-and-doomer, but he had a sense of economic caution."

In an interview with a magazine writer in 1974, Aaroe recalled how the Depression virtually wiped out his grandparents on the farm in New Jersey.

He also had a memory of a historic day when he was 14 years old. It was the day President Franklin D. Roosevelt closed the banks. Aaroe said he was standing on a town square in eastern Pennsylvania when the banks closed.

"Daddy didn't like Mr. Roosevelt," Anna Lou said, "but

I'm sure he got that from his mother, who absolutely loathed Mr. Roosevelt. Once I made the mistake of telling Anna P. that she reminded me of Eleanor Roosevelt. Talk about trouble."

Family members and close friends use to kid Aaroe about what a tightwad he was. He was not truly a tightwad, but he did not believe in throwing money around. He firmly believed in getting his money's worth.

"He was a fiscal conservative in every sense of the word," said Anna Lou. "He hated to pay taxes. He looked for every legal loophole in could find. His estate has all kinds of tax-free bonds."

Alden's distaste for paying taxes was expressed in a letter to Anna Lou shortly before Tax Day in the spring of 1965. He wrote:

"Don't tell Edna I told you, but I broke the 20-G [$20,000] figure last year for the first time. Me and Uncle Sam will have some settling to do. I'm about ready to go to the tax man with the numbers and see if he can whittle things down a bit."

As an avowed fiscal conservative, Aaroe usually voted for Republicans -- but not always. In the later years of his life he attended several state Republican conventions.

Anna Lou recalls a political discussion between Alden and her husband, Bob, about two months before he died. Her political leanings crept into the discussion and at one point Alden, wearing a disappointed look on his face, asked Bob: "Is she really a Democrat?"

Even so, listeners on WRVA had no idea how Alden Aaroe voted. He was a firm believer in not broadcasting his political opinions on his radio show.

"Alden firmly believed he should be apolitical and non-religious on the air," said WRVA's Lou Dean, who joined the staff in 1957. "He worked very hard to conceal his opinions."

If a reporter for the station allowed political bias to creep into his or her news report, Alden could smell it a mile away.

Some years ago, the story goes, Aaroe buttonholed a young woman reporter at the station and asked her: "Do you know what my politics are?"

No idea, she replied.

"Well, after one of your news broadcasts, I knew exactly what yours are," Aaroe told her.

Off the air, Alden had no qualms about speaking his mind.

"He was a more skeptical person than you might have expected," Anna Lou said. "He believed there were several points of view to every question, and he doubted there were any absolute answers."

One of Alden's frequent comments was, "I am afraid of the man who doesn't know he doesn't know."

Alden, Edna and Anna Lou lived in their beloved Little House from 1948 until 1954, when they moved into a new and larger house on their property a short distance from the Little House.

This time they let a professional contractor, Bob Fleet, do the work, much to Edna's relief, although Alden did insist on installing the plumbing.

When the county housing inspector came to check out the house, the plumbing didn't pass. Alden fixed what he thought needed fixing.

Back came the housing inspector, who flunked Alden's plumbing job for the second time. To paraphrase Robert Burns, the great Scottish poet, one could say that the best laid plans o' mice and handymen often go astray.

"Alden was so mad when his plumbing job didn't pass the second time," Edna said. "So he took a sledgehammer and broke all the pipes up. Then he went out and bought all new pipes and started all over again."

The third time was a charm. His plumbing passed inspection.

Their new house was a standard 1950s suburban brick home facing a new street, Henrico Avenue, that was cut into the woods off Ridge Road to allow a housing development.

The Aaroes dubbed their new home "the Big House."

Anna Lou was 10 years old when they moved into the new home. She had never had her own bedroom.

"I was so thrilled about moving into the Big House because

at last I was going to get my own bedroom," she said.

As the new house was taking final shape in the summer of 1954, Anna Lou became ill with infectious mononucleosis.

"I used to sneak into the Big House while they were finishing it, and go into the room that was going to be my bedroom," she recalled. "Mom and Daddy would find me there curled up in a corner with a temperature of 100."

Once the Aaroes were settled into the Big House, they decided to rent out the Little House. They notified the nearby University of Richmond that they had a house to rent to a student or a professor.

They landed a young assistant professor of mathematics named Ferrel Atkins, who became a friend for life.

Atkins was a native of Illinois with a Ph.d. from the University of Kentucky who taught at Bowling Green University in Ohio before joining the Richmond faculty in 1952.

For the first two years in town he lived in an apartment on Maple Avenue, but wanted a house to rent. When he left Richmond at the end of the 1953-54 academic year for his summer job as a park ranger in Rocky Mountain National Park in Colorado, he asked some friends to put an advertisement in the newspaper that he was looking for a house to rent.

His friends dropped the ball, so when Atkins came back for the start of school in late summer of 1954, he wasn't sure where he was going to live.

"I went into Dean Pinchbeck's office and his secretary told me about this unfurnished house for rent off Henrico Avenue," Atkins recalled.

"Well, I was footloose and fancy-free, and I could throw everything I owned into the back of the car and be out of town in thirty minutes."

In other words, he needed a furnished house.

He decided to go check it out anyway.

"I went to see the house and that's when I met Edna Aaroe, who was a most charming person," Atkins said.

Edna liked the young professor right off the bat, too, and decided on the spot that she and Alden should take him on as a renter in the Little House.

Atkins made an offer: He would pay extra rent if the Aaroes would furnish the house minimally.

Alden, never one to turn down an extra buck, agreed.

"They furnished it very nicely, and Alden provided all the firewood I could use," Atkins said.

Ferrel Atkins has wonderful memories of the two years he lived there beside the Aaroe family.

"We had a lot of dinners together," he said. "I remember one night when a bad storm knocked out the electricity, and Alden and Edna had nothing to cook on. They came over and we cooked dinner in my fireplace."

Alden and Edna played Cupid for Ferrel, who had fallen in love with Jan Hogg, a Westhampton College student from Hampton.

"Because the University of Richmond was a conservative school, it was an itchy situation for a faculty member to date a student," Atkins said.

Ferrel felt it simply was not proper for him to pick Jan up at her dormitory to go out on dates, so Alden or Edna drove over to the Westhampton campus to get her.

"We would bring her back to our house, and she would walk over to the Little House where Ferrel was living," Edna said. "But if she was spending the night out, she always stayed in our house."

Ferrel Atkins and Jan Hogg got married in Hampton in the spring of 1955, and moved into the Little House.

About this same time, Alden's mother, now retired from teaching school, decided to move from New Jersey to Richmond to be close to her son and his family. When Anna P. first came to town, she lived in the city in an apartment on Boulevard. Eventually, however, Alden decided it would be better if she lived next door in the Little House.

Alden had to ask Ferrel and Jan to move out.

"It nearly broke his heart to do that," Edna said. "I think he put off asking them to move for two or three days."

Ferrel and Jan moved into an apartment for several years

until Ferrel resigned from the University of Richmond faculty to take a position on the faculty at Eastern Illinois University in Charleston, Ill., near his home town where his parents still lived.

"We didn't really want to leave Richmond, but my parents were getting along in years and I thought it would be best to be closer to them," said Atkins, now retired from teaching.

So, the professor and his wife moved to Illinois. But it would not be the last they saw of the Aaroes. In the coming years, Alden, Edna and Anna Lou would visit Ferrel and Jan a number of times in Colorado, where Ferrel, the college professor, spent his summers working as a park ranger at Rocky Mountain National Park.

Chapter Five

By the time the Aaroes settled into the Big House on Henrico Avenue, a neighborhood was springing up around them.

They were no longer living in the woods.

They were living in a suburban neighborhood.

It was a stable, middle-class neighborhood with many young couples with children, and the Aaroes formed lasting friendships with their neighbors.

Little did these people know when they became Alden Aaroe's neighbors in the mid-1950s that their quiet little suburban neighborhood would become known throughout WRVA land as "Mad Mountain."

Two years after the Aaroes moved into the Big House, Alden got the break of his life from a career standpoint.

He was given his own morning show, the Alden Aaroe Show.

It was the break that would make him a Richmond institution.

It was the break that would make him the city's voice of the morning.

The year was 1956. Dwight D. Eisenhower, a World War II hero, was in the White House. Rock 'n roll music was in its infancy. The Dodgers were still in Brooklyn. And who knew the Japanese even made cars?

"In 1956, I was promoted to general manager at the station, and that's when we put Alden on the morning show from 5:30 a.m. to 10 a.m.," said John Tansey.

One of her father's favorite sayings, Anna Lou Aaroe Schaberg says, was one that he said many times in the course of his life:

"You have to be at the right place at the right time, and know the right thing to do."

When he got his own morning show at age 38, Alden Aaroe was at the right place at the right time.

And John Tansey was convinced Aaroe knew the right thing to do.

"I thought Alden was right for the job," Tansey said. "He

had a gift for making people think he was talking to them one-on-one."

In short, Tansey had a gut feeling that Aaroe had the kind of personality many listeners would like. His gut was 100 percent correct.

To understand what a break it was for Aaroe to become WRVA's morning man at that time, one must know what was going on in radio.

In the mid-1950s, radio was undergoing a metamorphosis due to competition from the new kid on the media block -- television. Instead of listening to radio programs at night, Americans were watching television programs. Indeed, many of the popular radio shows had become TV shows.

But everyone was pretty sure the mornings still belonged to radio.

"In the 1950s, it became obvious that morning was when people were still listening to the radio," said WRVA's Lou Dean. "The evening belonged to television, but radio still owned the morning."

To keep that morning audience, local radio stations throughout the nation hitched their wagon to a morning horse -- an announcer who would not be just another pretty voice, but a personality.

Aaroe became WRVA's morning horse.

And the horse pulled in listeners by the droves.

Several factors were at play.

For one thing, Aaroe had little competition. Richmond had only about half a dozen radio stations in the mid-1950s, and WRVA stood head and shoulders about the others. It dominated the market. Within the station's range, just about all the radios were tuned to 1140 on the AM dial.

But Aaroe never took his dominant position for granted.

"The guy paid his dues," Dean said. "He would go out and speak to any group, no matter the size, that ever asked him to speak. Alden figured the more hands he shook, the more listeners he got."

At one point in the 1950s, Aaroe's voice also was heard on

a small radio station that broadcast a religious program called "The Presbyterian Hour." Aaroe was the host. Although his Danish grandparents had been dyed-in-the-wool Lutherans, Alden's mother had taken him to a Presbyterian church in Summit.

His appetite for making public appearances never abated. Even after he was firmly established as the king of Richmond radio, Aaroe remained busy on the rubber-chicken circuit.

WRVA newsman John Harding, who joined the station in 1968 and became one of Aaroe's closest personal friends, said: "Alden's biggest strength, of course, was also his biggest weakness. He couldn't say no to anybody. And when you can't say no to anybody, you spread your time and yourself mighty thin."

In picking Aaroe to be WRVA's morning personality, John Tansey chose the perfect guy for the job. By all accounts, Aaroe's personality was perfect for his audience.

"Basically," Lou Dean said, "Alden was a disc jockey who visited with you, and he was exceptionally good at coming into your home. He would say something like, 'Well, it's a beautiful morning out there. I'm gonna have a second cup of coffee and won't you have one with me?'"

Aaroe's ability to make listeners feel as though he were talking to them in their home is best illustrated by the story of one female admirer whom Alden met at one of his speaking engagements. The lady told Alden that she listened to him each morning, but that she always covered the radio while she was dressing.

Listeners fell in love with Aaroe's informal style and his wit. An example of his wit was the time he commented on a news story about two young boys whose parents had washed out their mouths with soap after hearing the boys use profanity. Aaroe then dedicated a song to the boys -- "I'm Forever Blowing Bubbles."

Within a short time, the Alden Aaroe Show was the most popular radio show in town. It would maintain that status for a long time.

D. Brickford "Brick" Rider, who was WRVA's news program director for four years in the early 1960s, says Aaroe was
a pioneer in the movement to make radio announcers more
than just a voice on the air.

"Aaroe personalized radio and he was one of the industry's
early leaders to do that," Rider said. "He had the marvelous
ability to do radio in a way that was a one-on-one communication. And that's rare. And you have to remember that when
he started out, the industry was geared that way."

On his morning show in 1986, on the occasion of his 40th
anniversary with WRVA, Aaroe talked with Lou Dean about
his early days as a staff announcer reading news, weather and
farm reports.

"Well, we were program-oriented all the way," he remi-
nisced over the air that morning. "We were segmented in
fifteen minutes, or half-hours, or hours, whatever the case
might be. We had the Metropolitan Opera on Saturday afternoons. We had the Old Dominion Barn Dance with Sunshine
Sue. We had contemporary music programs. We had middle-
of-the-road music programs. We did lots of things and did it
all on a program basis.

"You [the announcer] sat in a small room and you had a
communication system, an intercom with a controller, and
they'd play the music, and all you did was read a script. Then
we began personality radio, and, of course, that's the way it all
got started."

The brave new world of personality radio was perfect for
Aaroe's talents.

"Alden had the ability to take his personal experiences off
the air, and make them into universal stories, or everyman's
stories," said Brick Rider. "He talked about his battles with
crab grass. He talked about pruning his trees. Or he'd say
something like, 'Well, we're redecorating the kitchen and I
spilled paint on the floor.' In other words, he talked about
things almost everyone experiences."

Once, when asked to explain Aaroe's appeal to so many
people, Lou Dean replied: "He doesn't sound like a radio

announcer. He sounds like the guy next door."

Aaroe had a firm idea in his mind what a radio morning man should be.

"People want to know things like, is it going to be warm or is it going to rain," Aaroe once told an interviewer. "They want to know what to wear that day. And they want to know the time. A morning man is pleasant and he has continuity."

Like everyone else, Alden Aaroe had his share of mornings when he was not in a good mood. To get going on those days, he once said, he pushed a "happy button between the eighth and ninth vertebrae."

Almost to his dying day, whenever he felt he was on stage and had to perform, he still was able to turn on the charm by pushing his "happy button."

He knew his show was popular. He saw the ratings. And there was no doubt in his mind why so many people liked him: He was a plain-talking, down-to-earth human being, just like the vast majority of people.

One of his favorite routines was to tell listeners what all was going on with his neighbors out there on "Mad Mountain."

"When Aaroe talked about the trouble he was having with Big Bad Bill and his other neighbors out there on Mad Mountain, people loved that sort of thing," Rider said. "He was human through and through."

One example of his "Mad Mountain" shtick was the time he was doing a remote broadcast from a storefront window at Thalhimers department store on Broad Street. Edna and their neighbor, Bill Bohn, passed by the window and waved on their way to lunch somewhere.

Alden told listeners: "Well, there's Big Bad Bill with my wife, and that's the way things are out on Mad Mountain."

Another example of Aaroe's ability to entertain listeners with chitchat about daily life was the morning some he mentioned on the air that he was going to be planting some bamboo in his yard.

The station was bombarded with telephone calls from

people who wanted to warn Alden Aaroe that planting bamboo would be a big mistake.

A few mornings later, an exasperated Aaroe told his listeners:

"I have never gotten in the middle of such a controversy in my life as I have with this business of bamboo. The other day, a very nice gentleman told my wife that he would give us some bamboo if I would come by and pick it up. Well, I was very happy to go by and pick up any kind of plant we've never had, and we've never had bamboo. Right away I began to get letters and phone calls. One fellow called me up and he says, 'Buddy, ol' boy, you don't know what you're getting into.' He says, 'All I ask you is come look what happened to me.' "

Aaroe never planted the bamboo.

By the time Brick Rider arrived in 1962 from WTAR in Norfolk to become WRVA's news program manager, Aaroe's morning show had been going strong for six years. Rider knew all about Alden's popularity and high ratings.

"I was just a young guy still kind of wet behind the ears," Rider said. "So I go bopping in there, and about my third day behind the desk, Alden calls me from the control room and says, 'I'm going off my shift now. Can I come in and see you?' I started sweating bullets because I had proposed several changes in the way things were being done at the station. So I figured Alden wanted to tell me a thing or two."

Alden walked into Rider's office and sat down.

"Can I shut the door?" Aaroe asked.

"Sure," said Rider, who was really worried now.

"I want you to know something," Aaroe began. "I've been in this business lo these many years now, and I've never met anybody in the business that I haven't been able to learn something from. And I want you to know that I expect to learn something from you."

When he heard those words, Rider became an Alden Aaroe fan for life. "I thought that was the most marvelous thing for him to say."

Like John Tansey, Brick Rider doesn't remember Aaroe

ever missing a day of work, and for many years his morning show was six days a week -- Monday through Saturday.

"He was always there," Rider said. "Some days he would come in with a horrible cold or an upset stomach, but there he was."

Aaroe was willing to do anything for the station, as Brick Rider quickly learned.

"I left TAR in Norfolk on a Friday and the following Monday morning they put up a helicopter doing traffic reports," Rider recalled. "The Atlantic Go Patrol, sponsored by Atlantic Richfield, which was doing that in so-called second markets all over the country. I thought it was a good idea, so as soon as I started at RVA I pitched John Tansey hard and heavy to put up a chopper."

Tansey bought the idea.

"After I got the green light to put up a chopper," Rider said, "I looked around the station and realized that of the 35 people working for us, only two of them knew the names of the streets of the city and weren't afraid to fly in a helicopter. One was me and one was Alden."

Realizing Aaroe needed to be in the studio for his show, Rider went up in the helicopter until the station could hire a full-time traffic reporter.

"I did the traffic reports mornings and afternoons for about four months," Rider said. "But there were several times when Alden went up for me in the afternoons, after he had done his morning show."

Lou Dean says it's a good thing Alden didn't have to make his living as an eye-in-the-sky traffic reporter.

"He was remarkably imprecise in his traffic reports," said Dean with a chuckle. "He would say things like, 'There's a red car stalled in the middle of an intersection, and traffic is backed up.' Listeners had no idea where the intersection was. Traffic reporting was not his forte."

Brick Rider also initiated a college football scoreboard show on Saturday afternoons in the fall that allowed listeners to call in and request scores.

The show was a logistical headache. A huge scoreboard, on which scores of games could be filled in with an easy-to-wipe-off paint, was erected around the studio so that the people taking the phone calls could see it.

"It was quite a production," Rider said. "And the first Saturday afternoon the scoreboard show went on the air, all of us were worried about whether it was going to fly. I looked up and there was Alden. He had come to the station to pitch in and help with the scoreboard show."

By the time Brick Rider left WRVA in 1966, Aaroe's audience was immense. It seemed everybody's radio dial was tuned to 1140 AM in the morning to listen to Alden Aaroe.

When it was decided the station needed a package of new promotional jingles, Rider came up with one that capitalized on Aaroe's popularity.

"I went to a recording studio in Memphis," Rider recalled. "We had to produce about 40 different jingles, so I writing 'em on the spot."

Thinking of Richmond's morning mania for Alden Aaroe, Rider jotted down a jingle that went like this: "Well, did you Aaroe this morning? Did you Aaroe this morning? From 5:30 till ten on one-one-four-oh!"

The station was good about promoting Aaroe, but he returned the favor by promoting the station in spades. By all accounts, WRVA Radio came first in Alden Aaroe's life.

"He was a team player all the way," John Tansey said. "He would do almost anything for the station you asked him to do. And he did a lot of things on his own."

John Harding said Aaroe's dedication to the station was never questioned.

"His first hobby was his work," Harding said. "When he was on vacation, he'd get up first thing every morning and call the station. Alden, in fact, worked just as hard off the air as he did on the air."

And he would go anywhere to speak to people in an effort to win them over as listeners to his show.

"Alden would drive miles just to talk to ten ladies,"

Harding said. "He never turned down an opportunity to meet people. He believed these people would tell other people about Alden Aaroe, and that's the way he built up this huge following."

Delivering a eulogy at Aaroe's funeral, Harding brought smiles all around by saying:

"Mark Twain said, 'Few things are harder to put up with than the annoyance of a good example.' Alden was WRVA's good example. If Alden could get to the station in fourteen inches of snow and sleep on a cot in the lobby overnight, so could we. If Alden could dress up like a reindeer and ride on a parade float during a torrential downpour, so could we. If Alden could go out on a personal appearance, get an hour's sleep and be back on the air at 5 a.m., so could we.

"The fact was, Alden always expected you to be better than you were. It seemed to have worked. Many of us who worked with him for so many years exceeded our own expectations. When we failed, which was often, Alden never showed anger or disappointment. That just made us keep trying."

His passion for work, work, work took its toll.

Anna Lou remembers getting home from school in the afternoons and finding her father working in his garden or his workshop, and then taking a nap before supper.

"I'm sure he had a life-long sleep debt," she said.

One of Aaroe's best attributes was his abiding compassion for people in need. He believed good deeds were important.

So when an officer of the Salvation Army approached WRVA in 1968 to ask the station to promote a fund to raise money to buy shoes for needy children at Christmas, Aaroe, then the station's program director, all for it.

So was his boss, John Tansey.

Thus was born the WRVA/Salvation Army Shoe Fund.

"The shoe fund was one of the things he was proudest of," daughter Anna Lou said. "And the thought that he might not raise as much money as usual last Christmas (1992) just drove him nuts. He really worked hard to push it. I had a hard time listening to him last year because he was overselling it.

He kept talking and talking about children with holes in their shoes."

The fact is, the shoe fund was near and dear to Aaroe's heart. Each Christmas he spent an inordinate amount of time and energy working to assure the fund's success.

And successful it was.

In the 25 years since it was established in 1968, the WRVA / Salvation Army Shoe Fund has raised a total of approximately $3.5 million. And there can be no doubt that its success was because Alden Aaroe asked people to contribute.

Listening to Aaroe's Christmas morning broadcast, when the check for the shoe fund would be presented, became a Richmond tradition along the same line as taking children to see the Miller & Rhoads department store Santa Claus -- Richmond's real Santa Claus.

The strong connection between Alden and the shoe fund was not lost on the powers-that-be at WRVA. When Aaroe attended a 75th birthday party for him on the lawn at the station's studios on Church Hill on May 5, 1993, it was announced the fund had been renamed the Alden Aaroe Shoe Fund.

Although the shoe fund was Aaroe's biggest and best known "good deed" effort, he solicited public support of numerous other causes over the years.

John Tansey recalls one of Aaroe's more intriguing reach-out-and-help-someone efforts.

"Some years ago, probably not long after Alden started his morning show in the Fifties, some teenagers in Highland Springs shot and killed a man's pigs," Tansey said. "Well, Alden heard about it, and he didn't like it. So he announced a pig fund for the man on the air. He quickly raised enough money to buy the man some more pigs. And that's just the way Alden was."

Aaroe could always find a worthy cause to boost.

When Hurricane Camille caused devastating flooding in Virginia's Nelson County in 1969, Aaroe asked his listeners to donate automobiles for victims whose vehicles had been washed away by the raging waters. Nearly 100 cars were donated.

When the Carillon, the bell tower that is a World War I memorial, was falling into disrepair, Aaroe helped raise money to fix up that Richmond landmark.

The list could go on and on.

Once Aaroe became established as WRVA's No. 1 on-air personality, his finances began to perk up because numerous businesses were willing to pay him to endorse their products in advertisements on his show.

Aaroe signed on with a number of these businesses, but he would not personally endorse any product he did not use.

"Alden was absolutely honest about that aspect of the business," Brick Rider said. "He would not accept an endorsement-type commercial unless he actually used the product and believed in it. He would read other commercials, of course, but he would not recommend one he didn't use. If he said he was driving a certain type of car from a certain dealer, you could believe he was driving that car."

Anna Lou said this type of honesty was important to her father.

"He really believed in what he sold on the air," she said. "If he talked about how great Toro lawn mowers were, you'd better believe he was mowing his lawn with a Toro."

One of the perks of his association with advertisers was that he often was able to buy products at a cut-rate price.

"Over the years he got a lot of deals," Anna Lou said. "This became an inside family joke. Any time Daddy bought something new, we always knew he probably got it for a very good price. We always nodded at each other and whispered, 'Another deal.'"

Chapter Six

When Alden and Edna decided they needed a bigger house, Alden wanted to stay right where they were, so they built the Big House next door to the Little House on the piece of wooded land they had bought from Mr. Gilbert.

His reason for staying put was because he firmly believed that part of Henrico County had the best schools. Being the son of a schoolteacher, Aaroe believed in the importance of good schools.

"Alden had been told by many people that the part of the county where we were living was the best school district," Edna Aaroe said.

The good schools to which Anna Lou would go were Tuckahoe Elementary School and Douglas Southall Freeman High School.

Soon after the Aaroes moved into the Big House, Anna Lou started taking piano lessons.

"Daddy found a wonderful piano teacher, Mrs. Doris Turner, who had taught at St. Catherine's," Anna Lou said. "And for the princely sum of $5 a week, I began taking piano lessons at her house. She was a grand lady whom I adored, but she scared me to death!

"Our neighbors and friends, Wallace and Ruth Bless, lent us their upright piano for me to practice on. We put it in the basement next to Daddy's desk."

As beginning piano students are prone to do, after about a month of lessons she became less than diligent in her practice sessions.

"Daddy gave me a stern lecture," Anna Lou. "He said that if he was spending this kind of money -- and $20 a month in 1954 for a radio announcer was big bucks -- and that if I was not going to practice and fulfill my end of the bargain, then that was going to be the end of it."

Anna Lou got the message.

"Forever more I practiced piano at least an hour a day, five or six days a week," she said.

Most of the practicing was done soon after the evening meal, when father and daughter made a beeline for the basement to get out of doing the supper dishes.

Doing the dishes after dinner was a chore no one wanted to do. After most evening meals, one member of the family would quip: "Oh, let's not do the dishes tonight. Let's just throw them out the window!"

One night after dinner when Anna Lou was 12 or 13 years of age, Alden had slipped downstairs to the basement and Anna Lou and Edna were facing the dishwashing chore.

"Let's throw them out the window," Edna said.

Anna Lou decided it was time to fulfill that desire. "I knew the three dinner plates on the table that night were the last three of an old set that Mom really wanted to get rid of," she recalled.

She walked over to the steps leading to the basement and yelled: "Daddy, I don't want to do the dishes. Is it okay if I throw them out the window?"

"Yeah, sure," Alden yelled back.

So, Anna Lou grabbed the old dinner plates, walked over to the kitchen window, and threw them out.

"The window was right over a rock garden," she recalled. "You can imagine the noise it made."

Everyone thought it was hilarious and the story became part of family lore.

But the typical after-dinner routine was for Alden to go to the basement and work at his desk while Anna Lou practiced on the piano beside him.

If she made a mistake, Alden would say, "Clinker!"

And sometimes he would hum the melody.

"Which, of course, guaranteed that I would mess up," Anna Lou said.

In his younger days Aaroe had learned to play several musical instruments: the bass violin, the violin and the piano.

One year at one of Mrs. Turner's recitals, Anna Lou and Alden teamed up to play a Brahms duet. They got off to a clinker of a start, at which time Alden piped up: "Well, we flubbed it, so we'll just start over again."

"I know Mrs. Turner must have been appalled," Anna Lou

said. "To talk out loud in a joking manner at a recital was something you just did not do."

Despite that inauspicious start, Alden and Anna Lou played simple piano duets and chopsticks together on many occasions over the years.

When other houses started springing up around them and families with children started moving into those houses, Anna Lou was very excited.

Finally, she had some neighborhood children to play with.

Alden and Edna were delighted to get neighbors, too, because they were not reclusive type of people. They enjoyed socializing with people.

Most of the people who joined them on "Mad Mountain" were the type of people who also loved to socialize.

"It was a wonderful, friendly neighborhood, and still is, for that matter," said Edna, who still lives in the neighborhood in a house across Henrico Avenue from the Big House.

Once the neighborhood became bustling with activity, a garden club was started. Edna became a member of the Glen Ridge Garden Club and even went to judges' school to learn how to be a flower show judge.

Edna's interest in flowers rubbed off on Alden and on vacation trips they began taking numerous slide photographs of wildflowers wherever they went. Edna worked up a 45-minute slide show and talk on wildflowers and gave presentations at meetings of a number of clubs and organizations.

They also became interested in birds, and one of Aaroe's most frequent lines on his radio show in the winter months was "feed the birds."

Anna Lou was responsible for converting the family into bird watchers. One summer, at her parents' encouragement, she attended Nature Camp, a two-week program in Virginia's Shenandoah Valley, near the small community of Vesuvius.

"I drove Anna Lou over there and left her standing in tears," Edna recalled. "But she had a great time and came home very happy."

Anna Lou, who attended Nature Camp for four summers,

came home raving about the joys of birdwatching.

"So, we all became interested in birds," Edna said. "Alden built a great big bird feeder and hung it where we could watch all the birds that came to it."

Two of their favorite couples on "Mad Mountain" were Julian and Philomena Bryant, who still live in the neighborhood, and Bill and Mary Bohn, who later moved back to their native Roanoke.

On Alden's radio show, Julian Bryant was "Sapphire" and Bill Bohn was "Big Bad Bill."

"It was never a dull moment on Mad Mountain," recalled Julian Bryant, a retired insurance agent who moved his family into the neighborhood in the summer of 1955, one year after Alden and Edna moved into the Big House.

Philomena Bryant remembers the time she and her husband went to Norfolk one weekend after their yard had been freshly landscaped by Watkins Nurseries. New bushes and new spring flowers had been planted all over the yard.

"When we got home," she said, "all our new bushes were covered with toilet paper. We knew it had to be Alden's idea."

One Easter weekend when Bill and Mary Bohn went to Roanoke, Alden recruited some other neighbors to help him play a trick on them.

"In those days," Edna said, "none of us locked our doors. We left them unlocked in case somebody needed to come in and borrow a cup of sugar or a bag of flour when you weren't home.

"So we all went into the Bohns' house and moved all their furniture around. We moved the living room furniture into the dining room and the dining room furniture into the living room. And we put a stuffed animal in each dining room chair, and jelly beans in the chandelier. I think Anna Lou even put jelly beans in their ice trays."

When Bill and Mary Bohn got home, all the pranksters were looking out their windows in hopes of seeing them pitch a fit.

But the Bohns did not take the bait. They went into their

house and did not come out. Curiosity was getting the best of Alden and Edna.

"We couldn't stand it anymore," Edna said. "So we walked over to their house and went in, and there sat Bill and Mary, as cool as cucumbers, on their sofa in their dining room. Mary said she was glad we had done all that rearranging because it gave her a good excuse to clean her house thoroughly."

When Alden and Edna left to go home, Bill Bohn looked at Alden and said: "Your day will come."

The Aaroes knew their day would come. They knew "Big Bad Bill" would get his revenge someway, somehow.

"We started locking our doors," Edna said.

Bill Bohn's get-even plan, however, did not require him to get into the Aaroes' house. He thought of a better trick.

Time passed and one Sunday Bill and Mary went over to visit Alden. Edna had gone to Yancey Mills to visit her mother.

Bill innocently asked Alden for a drink of water. When Alden turned on the spigot, blue water came gushing out.

Edna explained: "Bill had taken the hinge off our wellhouse door and poured some type of harmless blue ink in our water. We had blue water coming out the tap for days!"

Anna Lou's memory of the well is that was where Mr. Teenhoven lived.

"Danish folklore is full of elves and ogres, and Daddy, being 100 percent Danish, loved folklore," Anna Lou said.

"So we had an imaginary character in our family named Mr. Teenhoven, who lived in the wellhouse. He was sort of a cross between an elf and a troll, and whenever anything bad happened, Mr. Teenhoven got the blame."

When the weather turned cold in the winters, Alden always hung an oil lamp in the well to keep the water from freezing.

"But when I was a little girl," Anna Lou said, "he told me he was hanging the lamp in the wellhouse so Mr. Teenhoven wouldn't get cold."

Each year on Christmas Eve, they left cookies for Mr. Teenhoven as well as for Santa Claus.

Christmas, far and away, was Alden Aaroe's favorite holiday, which may explain why raising money for the shoe fund during the Christmas season was so special to him.

"Daddy just loved Christmas," said Anna Lou. "He would start dropping hints weeks before Christmas about what you might get. He really worked hard to confuse you with his hints, so that you were never really sure what you were getting for Christmas.

"The year I got the hi-fi record player that my heart desired, I thought I was getting a bicycle, because one of his hints had been that part of it was something that went around in a circle."

One year Santa Claus left Anna Lou a model train set. It was the first of four model train sets she would get for Christmas.

"Now, I never told Santa I wanted a train," Anna Lou said. "But over the years I got four trains. One year I was late to a Christmas cotillion because Daddy decided to give me a new diesel engine before Christmas Day."

Anna Lou liked her model trains, but everybody knew Santa Claus really was bringing them to Alden, a train lover from way back.

Those trains brought a lot of joy into the house, especially for Alden.

"As soon as we opened another train on Christmas morning, I would set up all the trains on the Ping-Pong table in the basement," Anna Lou said. "I would design the layout of the tracks, and we had a lot of crossings and tunnels and lots of switches. After I ran the trains for maybe twenty minutes, I would get bored and move on to something else."

When Anna Lou quit playing with the trains, Alden would run them around the tracks on the Ping-Pong table for hours.

The family observed one Christmas tradition from Denmark.

"For dessert after dinner on Christmas Day," Anna Lou said, "we always had rice pudding with one almond in it. Whoever got the almond won a prize, which had to be suitable for all ages."

This tradition still is observed in Anna Lou's home.

Aaroe's mother, Anna P., usually spent Christmas with Alden and his family when she still was living in New Jersey. Like her son, she also loved the Christmas season. Her method of fooling the recipients of her gifts was to wrap them in a way that made it impossible to guess what was in the package.

"When my grandmother gave me a pair of shoes for Christmas," Anna Lou said, "she put them in a hatbox. She also loved trick presents and practical jokes."

In 1956, the year Alden got his morning show on WRVA, his mother, now retired from school teaching, moved to Richmond and took up quarters in the Little House next to the Big House.

"Anna P. came to live beside us when I was 12 years old," Anna Lou said. "She was an extremely formidable woman who was at least 50 years ahead of her time. Very independent. Very intelligent. She had no interest in domestic things such as cooking and cleaning."

In short, she was not your traditional American grandmother type.

Anna P.'s favorite pastimes were playing solitaire and working crossword puzzles while smoking cigarettes.

"Always beside her chair in the Little House," Anna Lou recalled, "were a deck of cards, a crossword puzzle, a pack of cigarettes, and her smelling salts, because she just never knew when she might have a spell and get dizzy. All of us were convinced that she usually got dizzy at her convenience."

Anna P., who was hard of hearing, listened faithfully each morning to her son's radio show with the aid of a large hearing aid that she placed next to her radio. Always the schoolteacher and strict grammarian, she made a mental note of any verbal blunders Alden made on the air.

"If Alden mispronounced a word on the air, or butchered the King's English," Edna said, "well, when he got home from work his mother was sure to correct him."

In an interview with a magazine writer some years after

Anna P. died, Aaroe mentioned how his mother, "an eminent grammarian who demanded proper language in her house," used to chew him out for the way he talked on the radio.

"But I argued with her," Aaroe told the interviewer. "I told her when in Rome, do as the Romans do."

Numerous turtles lived on the Aaroes' wooded property around the Little House and the Big House. Any turtle they saw was referred to as "George."

"Anytime we spotted a turtle crawling through the yard, we usually would say something like, 'Oh, there goes George,' " Anna Lou said.

When Anna P. came to live next door, this caused some uneasy moments, since her estranged husband's name was George.

"One time," Anna Lou said, "my grandmother was standing out in the yard when Mom saw a turtle and said, 'Look, there's George!' Well, my grandmother turned pale and immediately asked for her smelling salts."

On October 4, 1961, five years after moving to Richmond to be near her only child, Anna Petersen Aaroe died.

A funeral service for her was held at the Frank A. Bliley Funeral Home in Richmond. Her remains were shipped to New Jersey for burial in the Petersen family plot in Oxford.

Alden, who worshipped the ground his mother walked on, was so emotionally wrung out that he took a week off from work.

The morning he finally returned to the studio, he crossed paths with Lou Dean, who was just getting off work after doing the midnight to 5 a.m. night show.

"Alden just broke down and cried that morning," Dean said. "It was the only time I ever saw him cry. Then he gathered himself and went on the air and got through the show."

One year later, death claimed the father whom Alden Aaroe never knew. The mysterious George Christian Aaroe died in Metuchen, N.J.

When George was dying, his sister called Alden in

Richmond to tell him that his father's health was deteriorating quickly. Death was imminent.

"We drove to New Jersey to see him at Alden's aunt's house," Edna said.

Had Anna P. still been alive, the trip undoubtedly would not have been made. She had shut George completely out of her life and out of Alden's life, and the son would not have run the risk of upsetting his mother by going to see his dying father.

The reunion of father and son was not pleasant.

Alden, who was 44 years old at this time, was at a loss for words. George was in pitiful physical condition and he was suffering from senility.

"It was a very strange affair," Edna said. "His father just sat there in kind of a daze, and Alden didn't know what to say."

The only words she remembers from that awkward reunion were words Alden's father spoke. Looking at Alden, George said: "He's a fine-looking man."

To this day, Edna believes the dying George Aaroe did not have a clue that the fine-looking man was his son.

"I cried all the way back to Richmond," Edna said. "Alden got so angry with me. He wasn't at all sentimental about his father."

Alden's attitude toward his father was influenced by his mother, who demanded his complete devotion and loyalty. She had pushed George out of her life, and Alden was expected to do the same.

Furthermore, Alden's committment to being a strong father unquestionably left him reluctant to develop a forgiving attitude toward the father he never got the chance to know.

Chapter Seven

When Aaroe started his morning show, he still was an officer in the U.S. Air Force Reserves, although his family and closest friends are certain that he never flew an airplane or had any desire to fly one after the war. Some believe he simply got his fill of flying in the war, during which he flew over five continents.

Even so, he remained in the reserves for about a decade. He attended weekend meetings and one year (1957) went to summer camp at Lowry Air Force Base near Denver in Colorado. He came home with a new hobby, photography, and a new geographical love, the Rocky Mountains.

"He absolutely fell in love with Colorado," Anna Lou said.

The next summer, Aaroe decided to take Edna and Anna Lou on a camping vacation to Colorado. It was the first of many summer camping trips the family would take out west.

"Daddy went to Sears and bought a great big green canvas tent," Anna Lou said. "When it was time to go, we packed our trailer and our car Betsy and headed across the country to go camping in the Rockies. It was a very, very long trip. Very hot and very dusty. And our car did not have air-conditioning."

The automobile that took them on that first camping adventure was a Chevrolet nicknamed "Betsy." Over the years, the Aaroes owned a succession of Chevrolet cars, all of which were called Betsy. The first Betsy had been a 1948 Chevy that Alden had bought second-hand.

Nicknaming the family cars was a practice for years. When Alden bought a green Crosley, a small British car he barely fit into, he named it "Mr. Petit Chou," which they all pronounced "petty shoe." In French, petit chou means "little cabbage," and the little green Crosley looked like a head of cabbage. Another example of a car with a nickname was a British-made Morris automobile, which they called "Mr. Morris."

When the family pulled out of the driveway in Betsy on that summer day in 1958 to head for the great west, their "Mad Mountain" neighbors were there to wave goodbye, including Julian Bryant Jr., "Little Julian" as he was called all over the neighborhood.

Little Julian and Anna Lou were the same age and had become like brother and sister.

"He really was like a member of our family," Anna Lou said. "He was always at our house. I'm sure he ate more of my mother's cookies than I ever did. He played with my trains and worked in the garden, and Daddy taught him lots of things, like how to drive a nail and how to split wood."

As the Aaroes pulled off for their great adventure to the west, Little Julian was one unhappy non-camper.

"I was waving goodbye to him and he was standing there with this hang-dog expression on his face," Anna Lou said. "He wanted to go with us so badly."

When the Aaroes got out on the highway, all they could talk about was how sad Little Julian looked when they pulled away. From then on, each time they went on a summer camping trip, Little Julian Bryant went along.

Most of the camping trips were out west to visit some of America's most scenic spots -- the Rockies, Yellowstone National Park, the Grand Tetons, the Grand Canyon.

"One summer we hiked Specimen Mountain in the Rocky Mountains and ate lunch on top," Anna Lou said. "On the way down the wind picked up and blew off Daddy's hat, at which time he had all of us sit down, hold on to a rope, and slide down the peak. He just knew everyone was going to be blown off the mountain. Little Julian and I thought it was really cool, but Mom still remembers it as being a very scary experience."

The summer they visited the Grand Canyon, Alden got everybody up in time to watch the sunrise. But they didn't hang around long.

"Daddy decided there were too many people."

Edna always slept in the big canvas tent, but some nights Alden, Anna Lou and Little Julian would sleep outside on the ground in sleeping tents.

"Daddy always said we had to count three shooting stars before we could go to sleep," Anna Lou said. "But he usually was asleep before he saw two."

One summer they stayed in the east and went to Acadia

Island in Maine and then on to French-speaking Quebec in Canada.

In Maine they walked through marshes and picked blueberries, and took an arts and crafts class in which they learned how to make wooden bowls.

"We all came out of the class covered with sawdust and just as happy as larks," Anna Lou recalled. "And Daddy's bowl, of course, was really thick and chunky."

In Quebec, Alden rolled down the window and asked a person for directions in French.

"We all were just dazzled," Anna Lou said. "I'm sure what he said was very simple, and maybe not even correct, but it was another example of how versatile he was.

"Growing up I was totally fascinated by this man who could speak French, quote poetry, play the piano and the ukelele, who was knowledgeable on a variety of subjects, and who also built a house, cut wood and fixed just about anything that needed fixing around the house."

Even when Anna Lou went off to college, a time of life when many young people have decided their parents are somewhat less than perfect, she used to brag about her father to her roommates and friends.

Not only did the Aaroes camp out when they reached their destination on these summer excursions, they also camped out en route. Except for the time they stopped for the night in the Great Smoky Mountains. That night, as Alden started to set up the tent, it started to rain. As she always did while Alden pitched the tent, Edna went to fetch water.

"When Mom got back with the water," Anna Lou said, "Daddy was trying to put up the tent in a complete downpour and everything was getting soaked. So Mom walks up cheerily and says, 'I got the water!'"

The drenched Alden was steaming.

"As I remember, that was the only night on our camping trips that we stayed in a motel," Anna Lou said.

On the trips to Colorado, the Aaroes always visited with Ferrel and Jan Atkins, the young couple who had lived next door in the Little House for a year before Alden's mother moved in.

When Alden, Edna, Anna Lou and Little Julian visited the Atkinses in the summer of 1959, Jan Atkins was pregnant with the couple's first child.

"I told Alden that if we had a boy, we were going to name him Alden," Atkins said.

That fall, in mid-October, Jan Atkins gave birth to a son and they named him Alden in honor of their good friend and former landlord.

When Alden Atkins grew up, he went to the University of Virginia and became a lawyer for a firm in Washington, D.C.

One year the Aaroes went to the Rockies early in the summer season. As always, they set up their tent near the house where Ferrel and Jan lived. One night a freak snow-storm hit the area, and it was one of those nights when Alden, Anna Lou and Little Julian slept outside the tent in sleeping bags.

Ferrel Atkins remembers looking out the window and seeing three bodies in sleeping bags covered in snow.

"I saw these three mounds of snow," he said. "I went out there to make sure they hadn't died from exposure. It was so cold that morning, they had to pack up all their stuff and come into our house to warm up."

The day before it snowed had been warm and pleasant, so the Aaroes had washed their jeans and had hung them on a line to dry.

"When we woke up in the snow," Anna Lou said, "the jeans were still wet and damp. It was freezing and all we had to put on were Bermuda shorts."

After warming up in the Atkinses' house, the Aaroes drove to a laundromat to dry their jeans. While the jeans were drying they went to a diner to get some breakfast. The diner was a place frequented by locals, all of whom were dressed for the cold weather in jeans and flannel shirts.

"So we go prancing in there in our Bermuda shorts, which these westerners probably had never seen before," Anna Lou said. "Needless to say, we got a lot of funny looks from the natives."

Aaroe always took along a tape recorder on the vacation trips to record his observations and mail them back to WRVA to be broadcast on the air.

Over the years, Aaroe filed tape-recorded reports from any number of distant locales -- from the Atlantic shores of North Carolina's Outer Banks to the blue waters of the Pacific at Waikiki Beach in Honolulu, Hawaii.

His description of Waikiki is rated by many as his most memorable remote broadcast. The year was 1961, when Alden and Edna went to Hawaii without Anna Lou and Little Julian tagging along.

With Hawaiian music playing softly in the background, here below are the words WRVA listeners heard Aaroe say from Honolulu:

"WRVA Radio on the go. Alden Aaroe speaking to you from one of the finest spots here beside the sea in the afternoon as we sit on the terrace and hear the music in the background. And out there before us, there it lies, the beautiful blue Pacific.

"You've heard it said this is the Polynesian paradise. And, you know, I think it's a pretty fabulous spot. I've been mightily impressed by some of the sights I've seen in this world.

"The heights of the Rocky Mountains.

"The great, deep mystery of the Valley of the Kings in upper Egypt.

"The history of Persepolis in the seat of the empire of Darius, and Athens, and Rome.

"But here's this spot that you just can't seem to forget once you've seen it. And that's the beach at Waikiki in this wonderful Honolulu in Hawaii.

"Let's paint a picture of blue skies and fluffy white clouds, and an endless, timeless sea, and the great breakers swelling and rolling and cresting into plumes of white, and tumbling onto this sandy shore.

"And out there, maybe a couple of hundred yards, are a couple of fellows. They seem to be just dots in the surf, lying on their surf boards, paddling forward, and, then, as the wave begins to crest under them, suddenly the board catches the front of the wave and they come to a standing position. And standing there with arms outstretched, what a fabulous sight it is!

"And, then, drifting lazily on beyond, is a schooner coming in from goodness knows where. In the portions between here and the reef, you'll see the skin divers, with their odd regalia -- funny masks that they wear, the tanks on their backs -- as they plunge down and hunt among the coral for various things that skin divers seem to hunt for.

"Here the temperature is always perfect. The sun is always shining on Waikiki Beach. And as we sit here and listen to this music, the East Coast of the United States gets farther and farther and farther away."

Since photography had become one of Aaroe's favorite hobbies after taking a photography course the summer he went to reserve camp at Lowry Air Force Base in Colorado, Alden always took a lot of photographs on his vacation trips.

Most of the photos were slides, because whenever he came home from a vacation, he and Edna would present a slide show to various groups.

"He did this free of charge," Lou Dean said.

But knowing how Aaroe loathed paying income taxes to Uncle Sam, Dean is convinced that one reason Alden always worked on his vacation trips was because his tax man had advised him of the advantages of doing that.

After returning from his first camping trip to Colorado in the summer of 1958, Aaroe sold Dean on the idea of making the same trip.

"Alden talked me into going on a camping vacation out west," Dean said. "Later that same summer (1958) I drove to Yellowstone National Park and camped with a companion, and the entire trip cost $86."

Dean was hooked on camping, thanks to Aaroe.

"He shaped my summers for the next 30-plus years," Dean said. "He always shared his books on the national parks with me and recommended places to go."

The year after Alden started his morning show, Anna Lou, who was in the eighth grade, worked as his sidekick at the radio station on his Saturday morning show for about six months.

"I didn't like getting up at 5 a.m., but it was fun," she said. "Daddy would let me select the music, so I would go back to the files and pick out the records. I picked a lot of Elvis Presley records and other up-to-date sounds. Many of his older fans called or wrote to complain."

Between records, Anna Lou chatted with her father over the air and helped him read announcements.

A youth reporter for the Richmond Times-Dispatch wrote a feature article about Aaroe's daughter working as his sidekick on Saturday mornings.

When Anna Lou was asked whether she wanted to be a radio announcer like her father when she grew up, she replied: "I get a kick out of being on the show, but I have no desire to make radio my occupation. It seems to me that anyone can talk and be entertaining. I want to do something to help people."

Looking back on that youthful statement, Anna Lou smiled and said: "I can't believe I was so dippy and naive."

The year before Alden and Edna went to Hawaii for the first time, Anna Lou turned 16. She was growing up and it was time for her to learn how to drive an automobile.

"We had a big 1952 Buick at that time, and Mom decided that Daddy should teach me to drive in that Buick," Anna Lou said. "The place I learned was the driveway that led from the Little House, past the side of the Big House and out to Henrico Avenue. It was only a one-lane driveway, so I learned how to back up very well. To this day I can still back up really well."

To teach his daughter how to parallel park, Aaroe rigged up two buckets with broomsticks in them.

"I had to park the big Buick between the broomsticks," Anna Lou said. "To this day I also can parallel park exceptionally well."

By this time, she was getting interested in boys for their

romantic potential.

"The first date I ever had was on a Saturday afternoon for a two o'clock movie at the Westhampton Theater," Anna Lou recalled. "When the boy picked me up, he had on a black motorcycle jacket, and, boy, there was a lot of consternation over that. Ultimately, that boy in the motorcycle jacket got a Ph.d. and became a research scientist."

Alden handled his daughter's dating pretty well.

"He generally was very nice to the boys I dated in high school," she recalled. "After awhile, I'm sure he came to realize what most parents come to realize. These people come and go at that time in your life, and you don't really have to worry about them becoming part of the family."

One boy she dated, however, did not meet Alden's approval.

He was a University of Virginia student named Alexander Britton Hume, whom everybody called Brit.

"Brit reminded both Mom and me a lot of Daddy as a young man," Anna Lou said. "He was tall and thin and had a very entertaining personality. Daddy, however, found him completely unattractive. He did not like Brit at all."

One night after Anna Lou had left the house on a date with Brit, Alden told Edna: "That boy will never amount to anything."

Today Brit Hume is a correspondent for ABC News.

In June of 1962, Anna Lou graduated from Freeman High School. It was time for her to go college. The schools to which she applied were on the expensive side: Duke University in North Carolina, Bryn Mawr College in Pennsylvania, Wellesley College in Massachusetts, and, closer to home, Randolph-Macon College for Women in Lynchburg, Va.

Now, Alden Aaroe was a child of the Depression and a man who watched his checkbook. But when his daughter applied to expensive private colleges, Aaroe never flinched.

"I don't think Daddy even mentioned what the cost would be," Anna Lou said. "He was so big on education, I suppose he thought if you were going to spend a lot of money, college was the place to spend it."

In the spring of her senior year at Freeman, Anna Lou visited the campus of Randolph-Macon College for Women. The dogwoods and spring flowers were in bloom, the grass was greening up, and the campus looked gorgeous.

"That visit swayed me away from going to a northern school," she said.

In the fall of 1962 Anna Lou Aaroe entered Randolph-Macon College for Women in Lynchburg.

Alden made one rule for her at college.

"I could not ride in a car on Route 29 between Lynchburg and Charlottesville," Anna Lou said. "He had driven that stretch of highway many times when he was a student at U.Va. and he knew it to be a dangerous highway."

Anna Lou abided by her father's rule. Anytime she travelled between Lynchburg and Charlottesville, she always took the bus or the train. Alden, the ol' railroad buff from way back, preferred for her to ride the train.

During Anna Lou's college years she received some 40 or 50 letters from her father. He wrote them on a typewriter at the radio station and most of them were typed on WRVA letterhead stationery. He often tucked in a dollar or two.

The first letter Alden wrote to his daughter, the collegian, was written in September, 1962. It read as follows:

"Dearest:

"So, one is in college. I have been thinking for some time what you would like to hear from me in the first letter.

"I suspect that right now something from home with love and affection is called for. As I write this you are probably driving or maybe lunching. But when you get it .. maybe Wed or Thur as you dash by a mail box .. you will probably need a little reassurance.

"As the time towards your departure got smaller and smaller I realized that you have some qualms and fears. Good. I thought perhaps you might take this step as merely another move in the game. But it is quite important, this going away from home. But you are not far away. The phone is so convenient and we would welcome you call as you would like to talk to us. Maybe we would need it more than you.

"You may have noticed the absence of 'fatherly advice' etc before you left. I've saved it for the next four or more years of letters. You'll get a little in each one. So here it comes for this letter.

"Ask yourself this question, and you won't get the answer for some time. The question: Which of my fellow students will become one of my best and dearest friends? Which one will become really important to me and influential in my life? And conversely .. to which ones and which one will I become important.

"Reason: Your college friendships survive beyond those you now have made. Your selection of friends, which at this time is the only factor over which you have any real control, is of paramount importance.

"Love & lots of kisses .... (signed) Alden."

In the winter of 1963, Anna Lou informed her parents that a boy at Yale University had asked her to be his date at a dance weekend on the Yale campus. She wanted their permission, and money, to travel by train to New Haven, Conn. The weekend would cost her about $100.

Alden wrote her a letter giving her their permission and full support to go to Yale. The letter contained specific instructions on how to catch the train from Charlottesville to New York, and how to transfer to a train bound for New Haven.

As mentioned earlier, Alden had made a similar trip by train in 1941 when he went to New Haven to meet up with Karl Alfred, his best friend from high school and college days, at the Yale-Virginia football game.

Alden's letter of approval also noted that he would pay for the trip, "and your mother will bring you a new dress to wear."

"Daddy was always good about buying me a new dress for special occasions," Anna Lou said. "In high school I could always count on him to spring for my prom dress, no matter how sensible he was about money matters."

There was one article of fashion, however, that Aaroe had consistently put his foot down on during Anna Lou's high school years: Bass Weejun loafers.

"Daddy thought Weejuns were outrageously overpriced, which they were," Anna Lou said. "He refused me money for Weejuns many times, until finally giving in and letting me buy a pair."

Chapter Eight

While she was still in college, Anna Lou married Stan Willett, a student at Hampden-Sydney College, near Farmville, Va. They had met while taking summer-school courses at the University of Richmond.

After the marriage, Anna Lou dropped out of Randolph-Macon College for Women and moved to Farmville while Stan completed his pre-medical course of study at Hampden-Sydney. She planned to go back to school later and get her undergraduate degree, which she did.

Alden and Edna were not happy with their wedding plans, but they handled it very well.

Anna Lou and Stan Willett rented a small house near the Hampden-Sydney campus. Alden, always the handyman, drove over to them get things squared away.

"He found an old washing machine with a wringer and a crank that I could do our laundry in," Anna Lou recalled. "And he found an old iron stove for the kitchen. I really think he enjoyed fixing up that house as much as we did."

In the middle of Stan's last year at Hampden-Sydney, Anna Lou gave birth to a daughter, Karen Cummings Willett, who was born January 21, 1965, Southside Community Hospital in Farmville.

"Mom came over for the birthing," Anna Lou recalled. "As soon as Karen was born, Mom called Daddy in Richmond and, by all accounts, he made record time driving to Farmville."

Since Aaroe had been away at war when his daughter was born and had not seen her until she was 18 months old, he wanted to get a good look at his grandaughter on Day One of her life.

Like most couples, Alden and Edna doted over their first grandchild.

"Anytime Stan and I went home to Richmond the first six months after Karen was born, all we had to do was hand her to the grandparents and we could take off and do anything we wanted," Anna Lou said.

After Stan graduated from Hampden-Sydney, he was accepted as a medical student at the Medical College of

Virginia, so he and Anna Lou came to Richmond and found a place to live on historic Church Hill.

True to her promise, Anna Lou enrolled at Virginia Commonwealth University to complete the requirements for an undergraduate degree. When she got the degree in 1966, she went to work for Richmond Public Schools as a teacher at Mary Munford Elementary School.

Alden's schoolteacher mother, Anna P., would have been proud.

When they first settled in Richmond, Stan and Anna Lou were busy with their studies, so Karen spent a lot of time at the Big House with Alden and Edna.

"Karen's relationship with her grandfather was really tight," Anna Lou said. "She called him Poppa Bear, just as I had done as a child."

Alden took his grandaughter on tractor rides around the yard, played games with her for hours on end, and they ate a lot of Edna's cookies.

The playful Aaroe always loved to play with children.

Former WRVA staffer Brick Rider remembers the first time he ever took his children to the station while he was working there in the mid-1960s.

"Aaroe was there, as always," Rider said. "He stopped everything he was doing, sat down in middle of the hallway, and talked to my kids like he'd known them since the day they were born."

On a rainy summer night in July of 1969, Anna Lou, pregnant with her second child, was finishing up her master's degree thesis when she went into labor.

"I was typing the bibliography when the labor pains started," she said.

By then, Stan was serving an internship at MCV, and was almost always at the hospital. Alden was assigned the task of driving Anna Lou to the hospital when the time came.

"Daddy kept his car's gasoline tank full all summer," Anna Lou recalled.

When the labor pains started, Anna Lou called her father

and he was there in a flash. They went to MCV and in the early-morning hours of July 20, 1969, Andrew Alden Willett was born on a day that made history.

Later in the day, astronaut Neil Armstrong became the first human being to walk on the moon.

One year earlier, in the spring of 1968, WRVA had moved out of the Hotel Richmond and into its new building at the corner of 22nd and East Grace on historic Church Hill.

At the dedication ceremony the featured speaker was Virginia Gov. Mills E. Godwin, Jr., who told a story that confirmed Aaroe's legendary status.

Speaking live on the air, Gov. Godwin said:

"I remember so well when I was in the Senate of Virginia a number of years ago. One of my colleagues then serving in the House had a visitor from down in our part of the state, a hundred miles or so away. He had been a rural mail carrier for a number of years. And every morning he had listened to WRVA and its early programs in the morning.

"He came to the Capitol, and he'd never been to Richmond many times. He hadn't been in a number of years. And my friend asked him if he didn't want to go up to see the governor. He said, 'No, I don't get to Richmond but every twenty years or so, and I'm not interested in seeing the governor.' Said, 'There's only one thing that you can do for me today. If you'll just make it possible for me to see Alden Aaroe, I'll be entiredly satisfied.'"

Aaroe's popularity was that strong. Given the opportunity to shake the hand of the governor or the hand of WRVA's Alden Aaroe, many Virginians would have chosen Aaroe's hand.

"Alden was our meal ticket," said Lou Dean, "and he was our meal ticket for a long time."

About the same time the station moved into its new Church Hill facility in the spring of 1968, John Harding was hired by the station as a news reporter.

"In those days Alden was not only doing his morning show," Harding said, "he also was vice president in charge of program direction. So, essentially, he hired me."

Harding, a native of Emporia, remembers well his first day on the job.

"The first day I came here, Alden took me to downtown Richmond to the corner of Fifth and Broad," Harding said. "We just sat in the car and watched the people go by. Alden said to me, 'I want you to sit here for awhile and watch people, because these are your customers. These are the shareholders right here, pal.' "

Harding recalls responding with words to this effect:

"Well, that's fine with me, Mr. Aaroe, because I'm from Emporia, and if I ever get homesick, this is where I'll come to watch all the little old ladies from my hometown come walking by on their way to Miller and Rhoads or Thalhimers."

After watching people walk by the car for awhile, Aaroe then drove Harding all over the city to show him where places were. "He showed me the town," Harding said. "Then he helped fine me a place to live."

The corner of Fifth and Broad was where Aaroe used to do the Streetman Street Man Show, a remote broadcast in which he interviewed passersby. One day, comedian Bob Hope, who was in town for a show, passed by. He and Aaroe chatted awhile, and Hope jokingly referred to Aaroe as "the man in the gutter."

Aaroe always was good about teaching the ropes to new staff members and helping them get off to a good start in their jobs.

"When he was program director," Harding said, "he took every hire he made downtown and introduced them to people. He believed in doing it the old-fashioned way, not with promos on the air, or billboards around town, but by meeting the public face to face."

Not only was Aaroe popular with the public, he was popular with his colleagues at WRVA because he befriended so many of them and he worked hard to keep staff morale high.

"Alden organized the staff picnics," said Lou Dean. "He

organized the staff Christmas parties. He invited staff new-comers to the staff out to his house for dinner parties so they would feel they were accepted."

Not to say that Aaroe was all sweetness and light around the studio. He sometimes yelled at co-workers if something went wrong. Some mornings he came in grumpy. But that should come as no surprise even to his most ardent admirers. It just goes to prove that Alden Aaroe was a human being.

Harding's first job at WRVA was covering the news at City Hall, which then was still the striking English Parliament-style building on Capitol Square known today as Old City Hall.

After covering that beat and other news beats for several years, Harding was brought inside to read the news reports in the mornings.

"That's when I started doing the early morning news in the studio with Alden," Harding said. "We worked together from then on and we became very close friends off the air. We palled around together a lot."

Harding's parents in Emporia, of course, were mightily impressed that their boy was working side-by-side with Alden Aaroe, because they had been Aaroe fans ever since he started his morning show in 1956.

"When I was growing up in Emporia," Harding said, "the AM signal was very faint. But we could listen loud and clear on 94.5 on the FM dial, because WRVA was simulcast on the FM signal."

In 1972, new federal regulations forced WRVA and other stations with AM and FM signals to separate their program-ming. So WRVA created a sister station, WRVQ-FM, which offered a rock n' roll format that appealed to younger listeners.

The first morning WRVQ-FM went on the air, Harding got a telephone call at work from his father in Emporia.

"What in the hell have ya'll done up there?" Harding's father bellowed. "Where's Alden?"

"Calm down, Dad, he's still right here," Harding said.

"Naw he ain't!" the father said. "I'm listening right

now and I'm hearing all this racket and it sure ain't Alden
Aaroe!"

Harding had to explain to his dad that WRVA and Aaroe's
show was only going out on the AM signal.

"So he started listening to the AM signal," Harding said.
"The reception was real scratchy, but he was willing to put up
with that because he wanted to hear Alden in the morning."

One of the little-known aspects of radio is all the shenani-
gans that go on in the studios. Radio is an ideal place to work
for a person who loves to play practical jokes, which was one
reason Alden Aaroe, a practical joker from way back, enjoyed
working in radio so much.

Some of the pranks Aaroe pulled over the years at WRVA
were the stuff of which legends are made.

"Alden was a funny guy and a lot of fun to be around,"
Harding said.

"To many people out there in radioland, he was a god.
They can't conceive of Alden Aaroe walking into the studio,
dropping his trousers and mooning everybody, which he
did."

The purpose of pulling a stunt in a studio is to try to make
the colleague who is on the air lose his or her concentration
and flub up on the air.

"People in radio often try to break up the one who's on the
air," Dean said. "It's kind of a tradition."

The goal of the prank is to be professional enough to
maintain composure. Grace under prankster pressure, so to
speak.

"Alden did play tricks in the studio, like everyone else,"
said Lou Dean. "And, of course, very few of his tricks ever got
talked about on the air."

One of the best Aaroe pranks Dean recalls was the time
Alden was taking a break in his studio while an announcer
was reading the news in the adjoining news booth, with the
two being separated by sound-proff glass. Aaroe squirted
some lighter fluid on the glass and put a match to it.

"Naturally, the glass window went up in flames, which

was very disconcerting to the person reading the news in the news booth," Dean said.

Aaroe's famous feathered sidekick, Millard the Mallard, became a regular on Aaroe's show as the result of a prank.

For some time before Millard got on the air, one WRVA staffer frequently would walk into Aaroe's studio and quack words like a duck in an attempt to break up Alden while he was on the air.

One morning in 1972, the duck imitator entered Aaroe's studio and started squawking words. Aaroe barked back. Both of them thought the microphone was off, but it wasn't. Listeners that morning unexpectedly overheard the first on-air conversation between Alden Aaroe and Millard the Mallard.

As you might expect, the telephone lines lit up. Numerous Aaroe fans called to inquire about that duck on the show that morning. Some called to complain they couldn't understand a word the duck said.

When John Tansey arrived for work later in the morning, he heard all about it. Tansey called Aaroe into his office and asked: "What's this nonsense about a duck on your show this morning?"

"Duck?" Aaroe said. "Nah. There wasn't any duck on my show. People must have been listening to WLEE or something. We wouldn't do that."

The matter would have blown over, except that when the duck didn't appear on the show the following morning, many listeners called to ask where the duck was. They liked hearing Alden talk with a grouchy duck.

Realizing that Millard would make a great alter ego, Aaroe approached Tansey and asked for permission to make Millard the Mallard part of his show. Tansey agreed under one condition.

"When the duck says something," he told Aaroe, "I want you to repeat the words so the listeners will know what the hell the duck said."

Aaroe agreed and Millard the Mallard became a star.

As the years passed, many faithful listeners became convinced that Aaroe was Millard. That was not the case. The identity of the person doing Millard's voice has been kept an in-house secret at WRVA, and it shall remain that way on these pages.

Aaroe was delighted to have Millard come aboard. It allowed him to add some zany humor to his show at a time when competing morning disc jockies were pulling all kinds of crazy antics on the air in an effort to increase their ratings.

Soon after Millard joined the show, Aaroe wrote a letter to Anna Lou, who was living by then in Iowa City, Iowa, where her physician husband, Stan, was doing his residency.

"He wrote to tell me he was now talking with a duck on the radio, and how wonderful it was and how everybody loved it," Anna Lou said. "Well, I thought he had lost his mind. I remember reading that letter and thinking, this is it, my father has lost his mind. He's talking to a duck on the radio. That can only mean he has flipped and gone over the edge."

Later, Anna Lou realized that Millard provided Alden a real outlet for his brand of humor. She even learned to accept his wearing a duckbill hat while he worked.

In the early 1970s, when Millard the Mallard joined the show, Aaroe and WRVA had some serious competition in town for the morning audience. Aaroe was now in his 50s, and other stations in town, particularly FM stations, had younger disc jockeys playing up-to-date music that appealed to younger people.

Aaroe no longer was the morning man everybody listened to, but he still was the most popular morning man in town, and ranked high in the nation.

A feature article in Richmond Magazine in November of 1974 noted that Aaroe had over 236,000 listeners each morning, a number that ranked him No. 1 in Richmond and No. 9 among the nation's Top Ten morning men.

The vast majority of listeners lived in Richmond and 32 surrounding counties, but Aaroe also had thousands of fans in Tidewater Virginia, North Carolina and West Virginia.

When the magazine writer asked Aaroe the secret of his immense popularity, he replied: "Let me give you a bit of my philosophy. What do I have in common with you? There are children, lawns, taxes, cold in the winter, sunburn in summers. I have something in common with a black man in Surry. I plant my potatoes on St. Patrick's Day and my peas in February."

Clearly, Aaroe was a man who believed in common experiences.

"He was always extremely proud of his high ratings," Anna Lou said. "The numbers were gratifying to him."

Many persons who achieve such a large measure of success in their field let it go to their heads. The wildly-popular Aaroe managed to keep a level head. He constantly reminded himself of one of his favorite sayings:

"Never believe your own publicity."

Like everyone else, he had his detractors.

"A lot of people have said Alden had a big ego," John Harding said.

"But I never saw it. He was the kind of guy who would just as soon go down to Surry County and talk to some guy in his cornfield, as to visit with the governor or some other bigshot. He was just the same with everyone."

One question that popped up constantly over the years was this: Was WRVA the most listened-to radio station in Richmond because of Alden Aaroe, or was Alden Aaroe the most popular announcer in town because of WRVA?

"There are two schools of thought on that," Harding said. "One is that Aaroe couldn't have been Aaroe anywhere else. The other is that WRVA wouldn't have been WRVA without Aaroe. The truth is probably somewhere in the middle.

"But I'm sure Alden would have told you that the station would have achieved its success if no one had ever heard of Alden Aaroe. He never thought of himself as being more important than the radio station."

Despite his popularity and the ratings to prove it, Anna Lou says her father always seemed driven by in inordinate fear of losing his job.

"I don't think Daddy ever felt comfortable or secure in his job," she said. "As the years went by, each year he would say, 'Well, they're gonna keep me another year.' As though that were in doubt."

Chapter Nine

In 1972, the year Millard the Mallard joined the show, things were going swimmingly for Aaroe at work. His ratings were high. His popularity was tremendous. He was on top of his game as Richmond's voice of the morning.

Things were not going so swimmingly at home, however. His marriage to Edna was falling apart.

By this time, they had sold the Big House and moved across Henrico Avenue to a smaller house they had purchased. Alden did not live there for long. He and Edna separated and he moved to an apartment in a house on Church Hill, not far from the radio station.

When they separated, both Alden and Edna were in their mid-50s. They had been married for 30 years.

On his radio show Alden stopped talking about Miss Edna and all the doings on "Mad Mountain."

"It was not an easy break-up for Mom," Anna Lou said. "But ultimately she and Dad became good friends again."

Edna concurs. "In the long run, Alden and I learned to like each other much better after we divorced."

At the same time their marriage was breaking up, Anna Lou and Stan Willett were on the rocks, too, out in Iowa.

"When Daddy began to realize he wanted to leave Mom," Anna Lou recalled, "he flew out to Iowa to talk about it with me. He arrived on the same weekend that I had made an appointment with a lawyer to begin divorce proceedings."

The divorce of Alden and Edna became official in 1974.

By the time of the divorce, Alden had met and started dating Frances Perry, a single woman in her mid-40s who was employed by the A.H. Robins Co. as manager of regulatory affairs.

Frances was a native of Durham, N.C., and the daughter of Dr. Russell Perry and Othello McIntosh Perry. Her father was a physician who years ago had purchased and installed in his office the first X-ray machine in Durham.

After graduating from high school in 1945, Frances had entered Wake Forest College, which at that time was in the town of Wake Forest, near Raleigh. She began college as a pre-med major with plans to become a physician like her father, but later changed her major to chemistry.

Frances graduated from Wake Forest in 1949 and went to graduate school at Duke University, where she earned a master's degree in chemistry.

After graduate school she got a job with the Central Intelligence Agency in Washington, D.C., and worked there for nearly five years before taking a job with a research laboratory in Milwaukee.

Frances worked in Milwaukee for about five years before deciding it was time to return to the sunny South.

"One year in Milwaukee it did not get above zero but four or five days in January," Frances recalled. "That was too cold for me, so I wrote a letter to Robins and asked about a job."

She got the job and moved to Richmond in 1961. She worked for Robins for 29 years before retiring in 1990.

Late in the summer of 1975, Frances and Alden drove to Florida for a vacation at the condominium he had purchased several years earlier at Hillsboro Beach, just north of Fort Lauderdale on the Atlantic Ocean.

Rolling along Interstate 95 just south of Petersburg, Alden asked her to marry him. For the second time in his life, Alden Aaroe had popped the marriage question to a woman in an automobile.

Frances didn't answer right away.

"We drove on into North Carolina," Frances said, "and Alden looks at me and says, 'You never have answered my question.' I told him I was still thinking about it."

A few miles farther down the road, Frances said yes.

But she didn't realize Alden meant right away.

Alden had a plan in mind. He was going to pull off I-95 just south of the North Carolina border and find a justice of the peace in Dillon, S.C., for many years a popular place for eloping young couples to wed.

Frances wasn't sure she was properly dressed for a wedding.

"I had on my black pants suit," she said.

But she did have her mother's wedding ring, which she had inherited when her mother died in 1951.

"I thought, at least I have a wedding ring to wear," Frances said.

And so, on Aug. 29, 1975, Alden Aaroe and Frances Perry were married by a justice of the peace in a very-busy wedding room in Dillon, S.C.

"After the ceremony, they wanted to take our picture in front of some plastic arches," Frances recalled. "We said no pictures."

They got back in the car and drove on to Florida for their honeymoon.

When they returned to Richmond, Alden moved out of his Church Hill apartment and into the house Frances had purchased in 1974 in Hanover County. The house, which had been built in the late 1960s, was located on a seven-acres-plus lot just north of the Chickahominy River on the old Baldwin farm property at the end of Cudlipp Road extension off U.S. Route 301.

Later, when a housing development grew up around them, the area became known as Craney Island Farms.

When Alden moved to Frances' house in Hanover County, however, it was isolated and quiet. He was living in the woods again.

"There were only about six houses out here," Frances said. "Our driveway was a dirt road through a cornfield."

"Daddy loved it out there because it was just like being back on a farm," Anna Lou said. "He filled up his shed with more tools and junk than anyone can imagine and he became very energetic. He was always renovating and doing things to the house. He moved walls and fences. He moved furniture. He added rooms, put in skylights and solar panels."

Aaroe loved tools and gadgets to a fault. He spent many a Saturday morning checking out the latest state-of-the-art tools at Pleasants Hardware, and often went home with a new one. The problem was, he never threw away any of the old ones. His collection of tools was a hardware lover's dream.

At the end of his life, his garage and tool shed were the repositories of his handyman treasures, including two tractors; two lawnmowers; two chain saws; three leaf blowers; two gas-powered brush cutters; two car trailers; a variety of power tools such as drills, saws and sanders; two spreaders, one clean and one gunky, and, the family swears, every screw, nut and bolt leftover from a project.

"Alden was a pack rat," Frances said. "He saved everything, including an old cement laundry sink that he removed when I bought the house in 1974, old cabinets and an old refrigerator from when we remodeled the kitchen, an old doghouse from dogs he used to have, curtain rods. You name it, it was in the tool shed or the garage."

Alden also owned many antique tools that had been his grandfather Peter's on the dairy farm in New Jersey. Over the years, Alden built sturdy frames to hold some of the old tools and gave them to his grandson, Andrew, as Christmas gifts.

Andrew inherited Alden's love for working with wood, and one Christmas he built a handsome chair and gave it to his grandfather. After careful inspection of the chair, Alden was most impressed and pronounced that it was a fine piece of work.

Alden, who often described himself as a "jack of all trades and a master of none," was always willing to help a friend with some kind of chore around the house.

One time in the late 1970s, John Tansey invited Alden and his tractor to his home to plow a garden. Alden couldn't get out there fast enough. The job proved to be a near-disaster. Alden somehow caught a finger in the plow while it was rotating and the tip of the finger was sliced off.

A nurse who lived two doors away was called. She said to put the tip of the finger in a bag of salt water and take him to the nearest emergency room right away. Alden's finger tip was sewed back on and it healed very well, but the finger was shorter and had a funny nail for the rest of his life.

Another reason Alden liked the Hanover house was that he still had a lot of trees to cut down, which gave him plenty of wood to split into firewood. One of his proudest possesions was a log splitter.

"It became his favorite tool," Anna Lou said.

The dirt driveway off Cudlipp Road extension came to the back of the house, so the first thing Frances wanted to do was close off the old driveway and build a new driveway (unpaved) to the front of the house.

It was just the kind of project Aaroe could get excited about.

About that time, Carl "Chuck" Yeager, the son of Faye Jensen-Yeager, Alden's cousin in New Jersey, came to live with Frances and Alden for a month while he found a job. Chuck had just graduated from Davis & Elkins College in West Virginia.

Alden recruited Chuck to help with the driveway project. They went out and rented a backhoe, and pretty soon there was a new driveway leading to the front of the house.

Frances quickly learned all about Alden's handyman exploits.

"He wouldn't let you hire anybody to fix something," Frances said. "He insisted on fixing it himself, which was dismaying for me on those times when I wanted to hire a professional."

She also quickly learned that Alden still was a farm boy at heart.

"The first year out here he tried to grow corn in the front yard," Frances said. "And, of course, the deer and the squirrels got into it. He planted four rows of corn out there, and I'll bet we didn't get five ears of corn out of it. So he gave up on corn in the front yard."

A neighbor subsequently allowed him to plant sweet corn on his property and Alden grew corn there for many summers. He loved having a garden, although some years he grew only tomatoes. With so many demands on his time, he did not have the time necessary to tend a garden properly. He battled the animals and the weeds with limited success, and by midsummer his garden usually was an unkempt sight.

He also enjoyed raising a clump of peony flowers from the farm in New Jersey. Family lore has it that the peonies had come over on the boat from Denmark. Anna Lou and her daughter, Karen, now grow the peonies that Alden and their Danish ancestors grew.

The same year Alden and Edna divorced, Anna Lou and Stan Willett also divorced. Anna Lou moved from Iowa back to Richmond with her children. Alden welcomed her home and offered to help her get settled into her apartment at King's Crossing, not far from where Edna lived.

"I decided I wanted to build these really neat beds for the kids," Anna Lou said. "So Daddy built a canopy bed for Karen and a bed for Andrew that had a step ladder going up to the bed and a play area underneath."

Later, when Anna Lou bought a house, Alden was always available for advice and help on fixing something.

Upon returning to Richmond from Iowa, Anna Lou went back to work for Richmond Public Schools. She taught at Westhampton Elementary for a year and Patrick Henry Elementary for two years, and then, in 1977, moved into school administration as coordinator for programs for gifted students.

One of the special programs that became Anna Lou's responsibility was the annual Richmond Spelling Bee. When she took charge of the bee in 1977, she asked her father to be the pronouncer of words. Alden, still a man who couldn't say no, accepted the offer and became the Richmond Spelling Bee's pronouncer for the next 16 years.

Aaroe's last bee was in May of 1993 -- two months before he died.

"He loved doing the spelling bee," Anna Lou said. "And he was very good at relating to the children. He made sure they felt at ease in a pressure situation."

Aaroe's willing participation in the spelling bee was yet another example of how much he enjoyed being around children.

Eventually, Anna Lou remarried, like her father.

In 1987, she married Robert W. "Bob" Schaberg, a Richmond business executive. Alden thought highly of Bob and and was delighted with the match. He referred to Bob as "a prince of a fellow" and they got along splendidly. They played a lot of gin rummy for pennies, with Alden usually winning the money.

"Daddy had a ball at my second wedding," Anna Lou said. "He even splurged and bought a tuxedo. His toast was the highlight of the event."

When Alden and Frances settled into the Hanover house in the mid-1970s, the surrounding woods had plenty of deer and other creatures.

"Alden called up a great horned owl one night," Frances said. "He heard one, so he just made the sound and the owl came and landed in a pine tree in the yard."

They frequently heard owls hooting and screeching for a number of years, until the Craney Island Farms subdivision was developed, at which time Cudlipp Road extension, which led to their driveway, was renamed Aaroe Drive.

Aaroe's favorite animals at the Craney Island house, however, were not wild animals, but the pets he and Frances had. Frances liked cats and Alden liked dogs, and so they had cats and dogs.

The first dog was a fat beagle, compliments of Anna Lou.

"When I came back from Iowa after my divorce, I had a beagle I had purchased in Southwest Virginia," Anna Lou said. "His name was Elmo. He was a 38-pound beagle with a very small brain that was directly attached to his nose. In Iowa Elmo had wound up in the pound twice, once for stealing a ham off a neighbor's porch and once for preventing another neighbor from getting to his garbage can because Elmo smelled something in the can that appealed to him."

Anna Lou could not keep this ex-convict in her apartment, so she gave Elmo to Alden and Frances.

"Alden and Elmo got along famously," Anna Lou said. "They took walks all over Craney Island and Alden loved to imitate Elmo's beagle bay."

After Elmo came two boxers named Cleo and George. Alden became extremely attached to them, especially George.

Cleo was the first to join the family. Frances had heard about a breeder who had boxers for sale, so one rainy Sunday she told Alden they should go take a look. "Take your checkbook along," Alden advised.

They returned home with Cleo, a six-month-old female boxer whose ears already had been fixed, and one less check in the checkbook.

"Alden immediately went to work building a four-foot fence around the yard to keep Cleo penned," Frances said. "Cleo promptly climbed over it."

George came next. Cleo was his mama. Both dogs had large appetites and would beg for table scraps. Alden would say "they have no shame," then feed them at the table. Their favorite treat was brownies.

Typically, Alden built a large, fancy doghouse with carpeting and a raised porch. But George and Cleo spent more time in the Aaroe house than in the doghouse.

George was a highly active dog with one bad habit. He loved to chase trucks, especially the brown trucks of the United Parcel Service fleet.

"I order a lot of things through the mail, so we get a lot of UPS trucks coming down the driveway," Frances said.

One day George was chasing a UPS truck and nipping at the wheels when the truck nicked him and flipped him over. He recovered but never chased another UPS truck. Anytime one came bumping down the driveway, George headed for the house. He remembered.

"That was amazing to Alden and me, because George was so dumb he flunked obedience school," Frances said. "He scored 20 out of a possible 200 points."

When a man offered $350 for George, Alden decided to sell the boxer.

"Why?" Frances asked him. "You like that dog too much."

"It's too good a price to turn down," Alden replied.

The man who bought George gave him to his recently-widowed mother as a gift. He thought the boxer would be good company for her. But when George tore up the woman's Martha Washington bedspread, the woman decided the dog was not the kind of company she wanted.

The man called Alden and offered to give George back to him. Alden agreed and went to pick up the truck-chasing, bedspread-ripping boxer.

"Alden walked in the door with a big grin on his face and George trotting along right behind him," Frances said.

Alden sat down in his favorite chair and watched George and Cleo get reacquainted. Once George had finished his joyful reunion with his mother, he hurried over to where Alden was sitting. He put both paws on Alden's shoulders and his face right in Alden's face.

"Alden and George sat there and mouthed at each other for several hours," Frances said.

George was glad to be home and Alden was glad to have him.

Several months after Alden and Frances were married in 1975, WRVA celebrated its 50th anniversary. The station threw an open house at its Church Hill facility and hundreds of listeners attended.

John Harding remembers that just about everyone who showed up wanted to shake hands with Alden Aaroe. One woman who was a longtime fan remarked that "Alden Aaroe was as much a part of her mornings as the smell of bacon frying."

Although Alden spoke on many subjects on his show over the years, many people always will associate him with one subject: Snow. He was the radio man who got to work on snowy days to report what was open and what was closed due to the weather.

Contrary to popular opinion, Alden Aaroe did not invent WRVA's school-closings announcement system, whereby school superintendents were assigned a secret code in order to prevent pranksters from giving the station bum information. That system was devised in the early 1940s, before Aaroe went to work for WRVA.

But Aaroe fine-tuned and expanded the system to include the closings of many other groups and organizations other than the schools.

Behind-the-scene stories about Aaroe on snowy mornings are legion around the radio station. In his tribute to Alden that was broadcast on WRVA the day Aaroe died, John Harding told one of those stories this way:

"Once when an irate superintendent phoned in to complain that WRVA had erroneously closed his school system too early, and being told that Mr. Aaroe would correct the mistake right away, the superintendent quickly said that if Alden Aaroe had closed his school a bit early, well, then, that would be all right."

When WRVA celebrated Aaroe's 40th anniversary at the station on Feb. 1, 1986, Roy A. West, a longtime Richmond school principal and then mayor of the city, dropped by the studio and went on the air to thank Aaroe on behalf of all the school teachers and principals and pupils in Central Virginia for all he had done to spread the word of school closings on snowy days.

"When we think of snow, we think of you," West said that day.

Mayor West presented Aaroe a proclamation from Richmond's city council, which had declared the day to be "Alden Aaroe Day" in Richmond.

Noting Aaroe's longevity, West said: "The years may wrinkle your skin, but don't let it wrinkle that beautiful personality that you have because those of us in Richmond depend on it."

In a lighter mood, the mayor harked back to Virginia's school-integration battles by ad-libbing a line that drew gales of laughter in the studio. Looking at Aaroe, West said: "You closed more schools in Virginia than Harry Byrd senior ever did."

Snow truly was one of Aaroe's favorite forms of weather. He loved to play in the snow. He loved to drive around in it.

And he took very seriously his responsibility to inform the public what all was not happening when a snow storm interrupted the daily routine.

"When he was home on snowy days," Frances Aaroe said, "he would say he had to go out and I'll see you in a little while. He just wanted to check the roads. So, he would take off with no snow tires and no snow chains. And he would just drive all over town to check on the roads. He had a radio in his car that allowed him to talk directly to the station to tell them what the road conditions were."

On those days when the weather forecast called for snow overnight, Aaroe many times went to the studio in the evening to sleep on a cot or a couch. He wanted to be sure he would be sitting at the mike in his studio at 5:30 the next morning.

There were times, of course, when a snow storm would sneak up on him during the night. But he always managed to get to work bright and early the next morning, no matter how bad the roads were.

"Out here, of course," said Frances, "his biggest problem was just getting from the house out to the main highway. Anytime he thought he might get stuck in the driveway, he parked his car at the top of the driveway. One time when there was a thick sheet of ice on the driveway, he really had a hard time walking to the car. He kept slipping and almost fell down several times. He finally got down on his hands and knees and crawled to the car."

After Alden and Frances married, they became close social friends with John Harding and his wife, Jerri. The two couples took many vacations together on the Outer Banks of North Carolina.

They always rented houses on these beach vacations, because Frances was not the camping type.

"My idea of camping is staying at a Holiday Inn," Frances said. "I react so violently to mosquito bites that I don't want to sleep under the stars. And rather than go hiking, I'd rather play golf."

The first beach house shared by the Aaroes and the Hardings

was a cottage at Nags Head. They liked Nags Head but when they discovered the beach at Duck, N.C., they started going to Duck.

True to form, Alden always took along a tape recorder and called WRVA each morning to file a report and ask what was popping at the station.

"He liked the beach and he enjoyed all the vacations we took, but he really preferred to be at home," Frances said. "We almost always came back from vacation two or three days early."

Over the years, Alden and Frances took many vacation trips to places all over the world. Their travels included visits to South America, Hawaii, Alaska, Nassau, the Panama Canal and a Scandanavian tour, on which they visited Denmark, where they hooked up with some of Alden's distantly-related Danish kinfolk and saw the place from which the Aaroes had come.

Alden's favorite form of recreation whenever they went to Duck was fishing, even though he never enjoyed much success catching anything.

"Alden thought he was a lot better fisherman than he really was," John Harding said. "Anytime we went down to Duck, after we crossed the causeway we'd always stop at a grocery store and stock up on groceries. One year Alden said, 'We're not buying any groceries for tonight. I swear to God I'm gonna catch us some fish for dinner.'

"Well, we checked into the beach house and Alden went fishing. He fished all day long. I think all he caught was one little ol' bitty flounder. So, for dinner that night, we drew straws to see who had to go get dinner. I drew the short straw and had to go get a pizza or something."

Aaroe may have unlucky at fishing, but when gambling for money he was as lucky as they come.

"Alden was the luckiest son-of-a-gun I ever saw," Harding said. "He loved to play hearts and gin rummy, and he wasn't a bad pool player if you played him on his table. He took a lot of money out of my pocket over the years."

Aaroe's competitive instincts were high.

"He was one of the most competitive guys I've ever known," Harding said. "He hated to lose. Could not stand to lose. If you beat him on the flip of a coin, the first words out of his mouth were two-out-of-three."

His competitive instincts served him well one night in the 1970s at a Richmond Braves baseball game at old Parker Field. The pre-game promotion was a hitting contest among local radio personalities. Aaroe was the oldest contestant, but he won the contest by hitting the longest ball. All those years of chopping wood had paid off.

Aaroe played all sorts of card games -- gin rummy, cribbage, canasta, bridge, poker. But his favorite card game by far was gin rummy. Flying home from many missions during the war, Alden had put the airplane on automatic pilot control so he and his co-pilot could play gin in the cockpit.

"Gin rummy was his game," Anna Lou said. "He was lucky and good. He taught both his grandchildren how to play, but he showed them no mercy because he hated to lose."

Card playing was one of the few activities that could keep Aaroe sitting still for long.

"He was not good at holding still," Anna Lou said. "The average length of any phone conversation you ever had with him was never more than three minutes. He always said that when you're on the radio, if you can't say it in one minute, you probably don't have anything to say."

Aaroe was especially adamant about dragging out long distance telephone calls, but this probably had more to do with his frugal nature than with his inability to sit still.

"During the four years I lived in Iowa," Anna Lou said, "he made it very clear that in our phone conversations we were not to discuss the weather. We weren't paying to talk about the weather, and, besides, we could read about that in the newspapers."

His social visits through the years usually were short, too.

"He was really good at the five-minute, drop-by visit," Anna Lou said. "About the only way you could get him to stay was to feed him. If you fed him, he'd hang around."

Aaroe had a big appetite and he loved to eat. He always cleaned his plate. He said he had seen people starving in India during the war and he thought it was a sin to waste food.

Peanut butter was his favorite snack food and it is said he never passed a jar of peanut butter without opening it. The potato was his favorite food, but he was not the typical meat-and-potatoes guy. He was willing to try creative dishes, which pleased Frances, a talented cook who enjoys experimenting in the kitchen.

Chapter Ten

By the mid-1980s, WRVA's Alden Aaroe Show was 30 years old and still flying high. Aaroe remained No. 1 in the ratings, and surveys indicated he was among the Top 25 radio announcers in the nation in terms of audience.

But the show had become a logistical nightmare for Aaroe. There were simply too many things to do and too many buttons to push for one announcer.

In the words of John Harding, "the show had become technically complex, what with special weather feeds, live traffic reports from airborne helicopters, lost and found pet information coming in by phone, satellite feeds, school closings, remote news broadcasts. It was more than one individual could handle alone, even one with Aaroe's experience."

Additionally, Aaroe was approaching retirement age, so the time had come to start grooming someone to become WRVA's next morning man.

In November of 1985, Aaroe took on a partner, Tim Timberlake.

Timberlake was a 1971 graduate of Randolph-Macon College in Ashland with previous radio experience at WTON in Staunton, Va., WRBN in Richmond and WRVA. He was 37 years old -- one year younger that Aaroe was when he started his morning show in 1956.

Timberlake's previous experience with WRVA went back to his college days, when the station hired him to work night and weekend shifts.

"The first time I applied at WRVA when I was in college, they didn't hire me," Timberlake said. "They put me through this gruelling audition in which I had to pronounce the impossible-to-pronounce names of classical composers and other words that you never hear on the radio. After the audition, they told me I needed to work on some things."

Timberlake then took a job with WRGN, a smaller AM station in Richmond, where he worked on improving his announcing skills.

Presently, WRVA called him and asked him to come back

for another interview and audition. This time he got the job.

In the summer of 1974, tragedy struck the station when the WRVA traffic helicopter crashed and killed Howard Bloom, the station's popular traffic reporter. Bloom's death tore up Aaroe. He greatly admired Bloom's work and counted him as one of his closest friends at the station.

The helicopter crash occurred just before Bloom was scheduled to take a two-week vacation. His substitute while he was on vacation was to be Tim Timberlake.

About a month after the tragedy, WRVA put up a new traffic helicopter with Timberlake giving the reports. Timberlake remained the station's traffic reporter for the next four years, during which time he also handled announcing jobs in the studio, including a midday show on Sundays.

"I got burned out and quit in 1978, and started doing all sorts of free-lance stuff around town," Timberlake said.

Five years later, in the summer of 1983, Timberlake got a call from Aaroe saying he wanted to talk to Tim about coming back to WRVA.

"My wife and I had just moved into our house in Rockville," Timberlake said. "Alden drove out to the house and we sat around the kitchen table and talked."

Aaroe told Timberlake he was thinking about hanging it up and he was looking for a partner who could take over the show once he retired.

"I'm thinking you might be the guy," Alden told him.

Timberlake was flattered and excited.

"I could not resist the opportunity to have the morning shift at that radio station," Timberlake said.

So Tim Timberlake, the former traffic reporter, returned to the WRVA staff in 1983.

"I didn't join Alden on the air right away," Timberlake said. "I helped him out in the studio and did some other things before I joined the first team, so to speak. It all worked out very neatly."

Tim Timberlake's first official day as Alden Aaroe's partner was the first Monday morning in November, 1985. The

James River was flooded by what would be called the Flood of '85.

On the morning of May 5, 1988 -- Aaroe's 70th birthday -- Timberlake arranged to have a former radio announcer call the station to wish Alden a happy birthday over the air.

It was President Ronald Reagan calling from the White House.

When Aaroe heard the president's voice he was stunned. Their conversation, which was broadcast on the show, went as follows:

AAROE: "My goodness, sir, unbelievable! Goodness gracious! With all of the things you have to do, sir, what a fabulous birthday wish."

REAGAN: "Well, I'm very pleased to do it. Do I have Alden on?"

AAROE: "Yes, I'm right here, sir."

REAGAN: "Oh, for heaven's sake! I was still waiting to be put on there. Well, I just had to call you as a former fellow radio announcer."

AAROE: "That's right! You started out in this business, didn't you?"

REAGAN: "That's right."

AAROE: "Well, you know, Mr. President, I applied for this job 42 years ago and I haven't had a promotion in 42 years, and look at you!"

REAGAN (laughing): "Well, maybe it's because I started earlier on the radio than you. I started back before the war."

AAROE: "Well, I did too. I got my feet wet in 1938."

REAGAN: "Oh? Well, but then we also have something else in common."

AAROE: "What's that?"

REAGAN: "Flew with the Army Air Corps in World War Two."

AAROE: "That's right."

REAGAN: "But I was with Army Air Corps intelligence and I didn't fly a plane. I flew a desk."

AAROE: "You flew a desk, yeah?"

REAGAN: "And I brought it in every day and never cracked up a single desk."

AAROE: "Well, bless your heart. I'll tell you, that was the five best years of my life, sir."

REAGAN: "Well, I know that this is your 70th birthday, and I like to call young fellows on their birthday. And as I see this also, my method of counting is it's the thirty-first anniversary of your thirty-ninth birthday."

AAROE: "I'll remember that. Thank you so much, Mr. President."

Timberlake and Aaroe quickly learned to feed off each other's comments and keep the banter going.

"Alden was very generous about letting me develop my style and my act," Timberlake said. "He never was critical of me. He didn't begrudge what I did on the air. I guess he figured he had hired me to replace him, and I needed room to fly. Which was fine with me, because I was ready to get some of the glory."

Timberlake even felt comfortable about cutting in on conversations between Alden and Millard the Mallard. One classic example of an Alden-Tim-Millard discussion went like this:

ALDEN: "Ah, here's a duck with an umbrella. C'mon, Millard. Water is supposed to run off your back, duck!"

(There's the sound of an umbrella being shook.)

ALDEN: "No, don't! Don't shake that umbrella in here. Aaawww!"

TIM: "We have an umbrella stand out by the front door for that."

ALDEN: "I'm gonna wrap that thing around your neck in a minute."

MILLARD: "Just a minute! Just a minute!"

TIM: "I guess the first question would be why would you need an umbrella."

MILLARD: "Now what a stupid question!"

Not only did Aaroe and Timberlake have different styles, they were dressed differently most mornings.

"Alden would come in barking at everybody like a dog, set his briefcase on a trash can, and he'd be dressed for radio in jeans and tennis shoes," Timberlake said.

"I'd be riding the board across from him within a rubber-band shot and I'd have on my television clothes, coat and tie, because I had to dress up for the TV-12 show after we got off the air."

Aaroe did some television work over the years, mostly appearing on commercials such as the ones for Western Sizzlin restaurants.

"He really and truly liked Western Sizzlin food," Anna Lou said.

The veteran radio morning man enjoyed the TV gigs, too.

"He liked the recognition it brought him in public," Frances Aaroe said. "One of the last times we drove down to North Carolina, we stopped in South Hill to get some coffee, and the girl who served us recognized him from seeing him on television the night before. He enjoyed that. I really think that if Alden could have gone back and started all over again, he probably would have gotten into television when it came along."

Even so, Aaroe spent his life talking on the radio, and it is the radio with which he always will be associated.

By the late 1980s, Alden was beginning to receive a large amount of recognition for his long service to mass communication.

In 1989, he was inducted into the Virginia Commonwealth University Communications Hall of Fame.

The following year, the University of Richmond awarded Aaroe an honorary doctor of humanities degree. Alden, who had dropped out of the University of Virginia before graduation to go to work for a Charlottesville radio station, put on a cap and gown and accepted a degree that could be hung on the wall.

In 1992, the Virginia Association of Broadcasters presented Aaroe the C.T. Lucy Distinguished Service Award, named in honor of the association's founder and WRVA's first general manager.

Then, before his death in 1993, the Richmond Broadcasters Hall of Fame gave Aaroe its Frank Soden Lifetime Achievement Award.

After his death, Frances Aaroe established a scholarship in Alden's memory at Virginia Commonwealth University, the Alden Aaroe Scholarship Fund for outstanding students in its School of Mass Communications.

During the 1991 Christmas season, Aaroe's favorite time of year, he developed a bad case of bronchitis. There was a lot of pneumonia going around that winter, so Frances suggested he see a doctor and get some antibiotics before the bronchitis turned into a full-blown case of pneumonia.

"We were scheduled to take a trip up the Amazon River in February, so I wanted his lungs cleared up and him feeling well before we left," Frances said.

Alden went to the doctor and an X-ray was taken of his congested lungs.

One spot was found on his left lobe.

Alden Aaroe had lung cancer. Grade 2, the doctors said.

The news stunned the family.

"It was so hard to believe, because Daddy had been reasonably healthy most of his life," Anna Lou said. "His biggest problem after he reached middle age was fighting to keep his weight down."

Upon learning that he had cancer, Alden was completely discouraged.

"He was really down in the dumps," Anna Lou said.

Anna Lou knew the feeling because in 1987 she had breast cancer and had gone through surgery and chemotheraphy.

"My bout with cancer was really scary for Alden," Anna Lou said. "He was greatly relieved when I recovered."

Alden finished taking the antibiotics to knock out the bronchitis, and in January of 1992 underwent surgery to remove the left lobe of his lungs.

The Amazon River trip was cancelled.

Alden bounced back from the surgery and returned to

work at reduced hours. In no time at all he was his chatty self again on the air. He was arguing with Millard the Mallard and yakking about the weather and telling listeners to feed the birds.

In other words, he was pushing his "happy button."

After his surgery in January of 1992, Alden had his lungs X-rayed every three months at the Massey Cancer Center at the Medical College of Virginia.

The pictures looked good each time throughout the following year.

Everything was clear in April.

Everything was clear in July.

Everything was clear in October.

And everything was clear the next January.

A year had passed since the left lobe of Alden's lungs had been surgically removed. There was great hope among his family and friends and colleagues at the station that perhaps he had beaten this lung cancer demon.

After the January X-ray turned up clear, Alden and Frances took a winter vacation cruise through the Panama Canal, a place he long had wanted to see.

Come spring, bluebirds showed up in yard at Craney Island. Alden, the ol' birdwatcher and woodworking whiz, built bluebird houses and put them out.

The warmer weather even got him talking about starting to play golf with Frances, an avid golfer. This talk of playing golf was astonishing, because the Scots' humbling game was the one recreational activity the competitive Aaroe never did master.

"The one thing he wasn't any good at was golf," John Harding said.

"There was a time some years ago when he and I went and played a Par-3 course often in the afternoons after work. We would chew up the course something terrible. The guy running the place always gave us some dirty looks when we came off the course."

Aaroe's inability to hit a golf ball with accuracy had caused

Alden to pretty much give up the game. But he knew how much Frances loved to play, and he thought this would be a good way for them to spend more time together.

Frances had been golfing since her college days.

"I started playing golf at Wake Forest on a nine-hole course with sand greens sprayed with oil," Frances said.

When she retired from A.H. Robins in 1990, she had encouraged Alden to join her for rounds of golf in the afternoons when he got off work at the station.

"But we never got around to it on a regular basis," Frances said.

In the spring of 1993, however, with the weather warming up and his duties at the radio station greatly reduced as a result of his surgery the previous year, Alden was ready to play golf with Frances.

Before hitting the links, however, he wanted to work on his swing.

"We started going to a driving range," Frances said. "Alden bought himself a new three-wood with a metal head. And he finally got to the point where he could hit that club pretty well. He felt good about that.

"He really was getting interested in playing golf when he found out he had this recurrence with cancer."

In April of 1993, Alden went in for his three-month X-ray. The pictures did not come back clear. They showed a little cloud.

"They did a CAT scan," Frances said. "And the whole story showed up."

The whole story was not pretty. Aaroe's lung cancer had recurred and it had metastasized. It had spread to other parts of his body.

Alden's doctor gave him four-to-six months to live.

"We all were devastated," Anna Lou said.

Chemotherapy was offered as an option, but Aaroe was told that chemo treatments would extend his life only a few months, and it would make him extremely sick.

Aaroe did not want that and neither did Frances.

"We said we didn't want to do that," Frances recalled. "So we decided the best thing to do was give him radiation to cut down the pain."

Anna Lou concurred with the decision to turn down chemotherapy.

"I think he made a wise decision not to do that," she said.

For the rest of April everyone concentrated on getting ready for Alden's 75th birthday on May 5. WRVA was planning a party and Anna Lou was planning a party. The party plans were tempered by the sudden realization that Alden was going downhill fast.

"He got really sick really fast," Anna Lou said. "Suddenly we all realized that this thing was happening fast. And there were many signs that Alden had known his life was winding down. For one thing he stopped buying clothes after his first bout with cancer."

Even though he was deteriorating, Aaroe did not stop going to work. He worked all five days the week of his birthday, which fell on a Wednesday. His last day on the job at WRVA was on Friday, May 7. He finished the show with Tim Timberlake that day and never went back.

At his 75th birthday party at the station, Alden was in great pain.

"He had a tumor in his hip that really hurt him," Anna Lou said. "The week after his birthday, he started radiation on his hip, which did help relieve the pain, but the radiation sapped his energy to the point where his heart started to act up."

Despite the pain, Alden pushed his "happy button" and put on a great show at WRVA's birthday party for him. He was delighted when Carl McNeill, the station's general manager, announced that the shoe fund was being renamed in Aaroe's honor.

On his show that morning, Alden asked Millard the Mallard to "put your bill right here and give me a nice big smooch," and Millard sang happy birthday to him.

When the birthday festivities ended and it was time for Aaroe to go home, he had to be helped to his car. The pain in his hip was so bad that he needed the help of a walker to move about.

Despite Aaroe's frail appearance, most of his colleagues at the radio station did not know how bad things were. They knew Aaroe was ill, but they did not know he was dying.

John Harding, Aaroe's closest friend at WRVA, was one of the few who knew what was going on.

"There was one day in April when he looked pretty bad, so I asked him what's the matter," Harding said.

"Well," Aaroe told Harding, "I gotta go down there to MCV and have one of those damned CAT scans. I tell you one thing, they ain't gonna cut on me anymore, and I'm not gonna do this chemotherapy stuff."

At the 75th birthday party, Harding knew his friend was slipping away.

"By that time, Alden was really slowing down," Harding said. "He had to use a walker to get around, because his hip was hurting so much. We didn't talk about it that day, but I knew it was a matter of time. He took the next week off and he never came back to work.

"He did come back to the station one time, but he just sat out in the car. I went out there to talk to him and Alden said, 'You know what the score is don't you, buddy?' I said yeah. But he didn't want to come into the station and talk about it with everybody."

Chapter Eleven

The week after his 75th birthday party, Alden Aaroe began radiation treatment on his hip at MCV's Massey Cancer Center. It relieved the pain but made him weak.

Two weeks later, on Monday, May 24, he checked into the hospital at MCV. The radiation treatments had taken away his appetite and sapped what little energy he had left in his body.

On Thursday, WRVA's Lou Dean called Alden in the hospital and conducted a tape-recorded interview to be played that evening on Dean's show. Alden agreed with Lou that his countless fans on WRVA deserved to be updated on his situation.

Aaroe's voice sounded upbeat in the interview that was broadcast, but it was evident he had accepted his own mortality.

When Lou informed Aaroe that the station had been getting many telephone calls from listeners inquiring about Aaroe's health, Alden said: "Well, I appreciate that. You gotta stop and look at it though. I am 75. And I've had 75 wonderful years. And I knew that one day the voice and the rest of the human body would have to give out. Gimme a year. Gimme six months or whatever."

Aaroe assured listeners he was "as comfortable as I can feel" and that all he could do was "hope for the best" in his goal "to be as little trouble to anybody, myself included, and still get the benefits of home and the medical care that's available."

The interview concluded with Aaroe saying: "That's the best I can give you right now, Lou, and we'll talk next week."

After completing the interview for the public, Dean asked Aaroe to say something to the WRVA staff on tape. Aaroe's voice in the message to his colleagues was not as upbeat as it had been for his fans.

"Hi there," Alden began. "Boy, I'll tell you. I've been having a bad time of it and I guess some of you have been wondering what in the world's going on."

After explaining his medical situation in some detail, Alden said: "I somehow sort of doubt that I'll be back on the air ever. I wish it weren't so, but that's the way it appears to me at this time."

He was saying goodbye to WRVA.

Aaroe received a number of visitors while he was in the hospital in the final days of May and early June.

His cousin, Faye Jensen-Yeager, drove down from New Jersey. She and Alden talked about the farm and he said how much he wished he could visit the old homestead one more time.

Muty Yurachek, whom he had met while stationed in Iran in World War II, dropped by unexpectedly and they chatted about the war years.

A surprise visitor was Alden Atkins, the son of Ferrel and Jan Atkins, the couple who had lived in the Little House. Now a lawyer in Washington, D.C., young Alden wanted to see the man for whom he had been named.

"Alden Atkins and Daddy talked for about an hour," Anna Lou said. "Daddy told him a lot of things about his Air Force days and a lot of things about his life. It was astonishing."

From his hospital room Alden called Dr. Karl Alfred, his best friend from high school and college days. They had a good conversation about the days when they were young.

Alden used a tape recorder to record some thoughts about his life and he called his family members and some of his closest friends together to listen to it.

After several days in the hospital, Alden's heart started acting up. When his heartbeat stabilized, he felt slightly better, but he began to show signs of mental deterioration caused by a tumor in his spinal cord.

By the Memorial Day holiday weekend, Alden's doctor told the family that time was running out. They started planning a funeral service.

Alden's grandson, Andrew Willett, drove over from Virginia Tech University in Blacksburg to visit.

"Andrew had a good visit in which Daddy apparently spoke to him about now that he was ready to graduate from college, it was the time to seize life and show what he could do," Anna Lou said. "Andrew came out of the room in tears. Daddy checked with me to see that it was okay for him to have given Andrew a motivational talk. I said it was okay."

During one of her moments with her father in the hospital, Anna Lou and Alden sang "Tit Willow" from The Mikado, the Gilbert and Sullivan operetta. Aaroe loved Gilbert and Sullivan and he loved opera. Over the years he had spent many a Saturday tinkering in his workshop and listening to a Metropolitan Opera program on the radio.

One night when they were watching the news on television, Alden paid close attention to a report about fighting in Bosnia. Turning to Anna Lou, he remarked: "Do you think there will ever be an end to war?"

She suspected this question had been on his "worry list" a long time.

One day in early June, Alden asked his doctor: "Can't we just cut all this stuff out?" His doctor agreed. Radiation was stopped and Aaroe was taken off the heart-monitoring machine. Everyone assumed he soon would die in the hospital.

Instead, he perked up.

One morning, Anna Lou walked into his hospital room. Alden, looking somewhat chipper, annnounced: "I've decided I'm not going to die and I'm going home."

And so he went home. It was early June. The bluebirds were living in the houses he had built.

Alden Aaroe spent the last five weeks in the Hanover County home where he and Frances had lived for 18 years.

Frances took charge and did a wonderful job of organizing his care. She set up the den to be Alden's hospital room. She coordinated round-the-clock nursing shifts, handled the many phone calls and the get-well cards that filled two shopping bags. She wanted to keep Alden as comfortable as possible and enable him to get plenty of rest. Yet, at the same time, she managed for all his visitors to have some time with him.

"He spent most of the time in his pajamas because he slept a lot," Anna Lou said. "But there were days he would dress and we could sit arond and talk about things."

A steady stream of visitors came to the house.

"It was amazing to see him perk up when he recognized them," Anna Lou said. "He would be lying there half asleep, and somebody would walk in, and we would say, 'Alden, so-and-so is here to see you.' And he would just light up and start talking away as though nothing was wrong. He had lost the voice, but he could still push that radio happy button and turn it on when he wanted to."

One day in late June, Carl Stutz, who had worked with Alden at WRVA in the 1950s, telephoned. Alden took the receiver and said: "Hi, Carl! How ya been? Well, I don't eat enough, my daughter says."

Anna Lou shook her head and thought: "Is this the same man who hasn't spoken two clear words all day."

Among the visitors was Little Julian Bryant, the kid from "Mad Mountain" and now a lawyer in Virginia Beach. He wanted to see the man who had taught him how to drive a nail and pitch a camping tent.

Little Julian's parents, Julian and Philomena Bryant, also visited several times from the old neighborhood.

Harvey Hudson, who had been WLEE's top radio announcer and Aaroe's main competitor for many years, visited a number of times.

Bob Fleet, the contractor who had built the Big House, paid several calls.

Alden's grandaughter, Karen, flew in from Little Rock, Ark., to be there. Andrew, the grandson, telephoned to say he was caught up in the middle of finishing his thesis for a bachelor's degree in architecture at Virginia Tech, and would be over for a visit as soon as he completed the task.

Alden and Andrew had a long talk on the telephone and Alden gave his grandson some advice: "Andrew, these are your last days in school there. Go find a wooden beam somewhere and carve your initials in it so that forty years from now you can go back and laugh and cry and remember."

The radio station sent food and the mail each day until Frances had to tell them the food was overwhelming them.

The deliveries were cut back to every other day.

Rick Kalkofen, a close friend of Alden and Frances, promised Alden that he would stay by his bed at nights, which he did. Rick also was there often during the day. One day when Alden felt like going outside but could not walk, Rick hooked up a wagon to the tractor and gave Alden a spin around the yard. The pin came unhooked and Alden was dumped out of the wagon and into the grass. Everybody laughed, including Alden.

Edna, his first wife, was there almost every day, too.

"Mom would sit by his bed and they would talk," Anna Lou. "Daddy and Mom had great closure."

On good days, Alden liked to sit on the porch with Frances and look at the trees and any birds that might fly by. Good days were porch days.

All his life Alden had enjoyed being outdoors. A tramp in the woods with his dogs was a routine part of his existence until trouble with his knees made walking a painful act. He loved the countryside and the change of seasons.

One warm afternoon on a good day, Alden went out to the porch to sit a spell. Anna Lou threw open a window and sat down at the piano to play for him.

"I made some clinkers, just like I always had done when I was a little girl practicing at the piano beside his desk," Anna Lou said.

Presently, Alden came into the house and sat down beside her at the piano. Together, father and daughter played their famous rendition of Chopsticks.

Alden Aaroe was performing to the very end.

"Frances and I have talked about this a lot," Anna Lou said. "We think he just wanted to go out in character. Some of the things he did near the end were acts of loving closure with people, and some of it was his way of saying I want you to remember me as the person I was."

The last few days were grim.

"Daddy couldn't talk," Anna Lou said. "The voice was gone."

To control the pain in his body, morphine was being fed intravenously into his veins.

Toward the end he had some dreams about flying.

"You could see him holding the wheel and flipping the controls," Anna Lou said. "Once he woke up and asked what the altitude was. We all got in the habit of going along with the conversation."

His last visitor was John Tansey, his longtime friend and the man who had hired him at WRVA in 1946 for an extra $25 a month.

It was not a good visit.

"I went out to see Alden at his house the day before he died," Tansey said. "He couldn't see and he couldn't talk. I said out loud, 'Well, I'm going to leave now.' Alden must have heard that because after I had left his bedside, somebody called me back. I went back and held Alden's arm. I just held his arm awhile and tried to communicate with him by touch. And that was the last I saw of him."

In the early morning hours of Wednesday, July 7, 1993, Alden Aaroe died in the bedroom of the house at the end of Aaroe Drive in Hanover County. The time of death was 2:50 a.m., about an hour earlier than the time of day he had arisen for many years to go to work as WRVA's morning man.

Frances had gone to bed about an hour earlier.

Anna Lou was curled up on a sofa across from her father's bed.

Rick Kalkofen was sitting beside his bed at the moment of death.

When Rick saw that Alden had stopped breathing, he shook Anna Lou awake. She went to the bed and told her father goodbye. Rick and Anna Lou then woke up Frances, and the three of them stood together by the bed and had a good cry.

Presently, they called the Hospice nurse, Edna, Anna Lou's husband Bob, and the radio station.

Around 5 a.m. they switched on the radio to see what would be reported.

Aaroe's obituary was not in the Richmond Times-Dispatch that morning because the time of his death came after the newpaper's final Wednesday edition had gone to press.

It was fitting that the news of Alden Aaroe's death was delivered first to the public over WRVA Radio.

Throughout the day, WRVA broadcast tributes to Aaroe, and many listeners called to share their memories of the man over the air. It was a trip down memory lane.

"I just lay curled up on the sofa listening all morning," Anna Lou said. "It was amazing. They had prepared a wonderful collection of old clips and they played many of the promotional jingles I remembered so well. The phone calls from listeners were wonderful and included so many stories we didn't know. We all felt lifted up by the entire city. It was like a big wave of love. All of us were touched, and it went on all day. It was just incredible. And John Harding's 30-minute memorial piece was simply fantastic."

That night, Ferrel and Jan Atkins, the couple who had once lived in the Little House, tuned into WRVA at their home in Illinois. Through the power of 50,000 watts, they heard some of the tributes to the landlord for whom they had named their son.

Aaroe's death made front-page news in Thursday's Times-Dispatch. The obituary started on Page One and was continued inside for a total of more than 40 inches in length. It was accompanied by three photographs, including one of Alden with George and Cleo, the boxers he had loved so much.

The obituary's headline read: "Voice of the morning falls silent."

A memorial service was held the following Saturday afternoon at St. Paul's Episcopal Church in downtown Richmond, across East Grace Street from the old Hotel Richmond where Aaroe had started his career at WRVA.

The service, presided over by The Rev. Canon Robert G. Heatherington and broadcast over WRVA, was a celebration of Aaroe's long and productive life.

The congregation, large in number, sang "For the Beauty

of the Earth," and a gospel group, The Silver Stars, longtime performers on WRVA on Sunday mornings, sang "Amazing Grace."

Tim Timberlake read selected passages from the Bible and Anna Lou told a story about her father and a blind man.

Many years ago, the story goes, Alden was in Petersburg and was asked to visit a man who wanted to meet him. When Alden shook his hand, the man said: "Mr. Aaroe, I am blind, and when I listen to you, you are my eyes."

Aaroe, who always had been a great proponent of the importance of theater of the mind, considered it the greatest compliment he ever received.

John Harding deliver the eulogy.

"I don't want you to do a traditional eulogy," Anna Lou had told him before the service. "I want you to have some fun, without going overboard, of course. Remember, this is going to be in St. Paul's!"

Harding began his eulogy by saying: "Having friends takes time. Alden Aaroe, who's life we are celebrating today, had tens of thousands of friends because he made the time for them."

Here below are other excerpts:

"Generations of listeners grew up with Alden on the radio. Many of those who moved away from Richmond and Virginia still kept in touch via WRVA's strong signal. A few minutes with Alden on the radio was like a trip back home. You could almost smell the bacon frying, and remember hoping beyond hope on snowy mornings that Mr. Aaroe would close your school."

"But even good examples have their lapses and so did Alden. He wasn't above putting a picture of Millard the Mallard on his undershorts, and did. And took great pleasure in personally modeling his handiwork in the studio. Good thing it was radio."

"I recall a visit from Alden and Frances soon after my wife, Jerri, and I moved into our new home in Chesterfield County. Alden peered out a back window and wondered where I

Voice of the Morning

149

intended to put our clothesline. I responded that we weren't allowed to have a clothesline. Aaroe was incredulous. What do you mean you can't have a clothesline? All homes have a clothesline! The subject was dropped until one morning we noticed a makeshift clothesline strung around the backyard decorated with very suspicious underwear. Size extra large. Including one pair of very large undershorts with a picture of Millard the Mallard on the seat."

"He was a confident person but never cocky. Years ago, we were fishing on the Chesapeake Bay. I brought along my nephew Paul. The big rod and reel proved too much for Paul and it slipped from his hands and plunged to the bottom. Alden got him another one and said, 'Don't worry, Paul, we'll get it back.' An hour or so later, Alden walked aft with the lost rod and reel. He had fished it up from the bottom. When I asked him how he managed to pull that off, he said, 'John, believe me, I'd much rather have caught a fish.'"

The service closed with the Gaelic Blessing that begins, "May the road rise to meet you," which Aaroe frequently quoted, and a singing of the hymn "Joyful, Joyful."

After the service, John Harding shook hands with Rev. Heatherington.

"Well," Harding said, "I guess this is the first time anybody ever talked about underwear in St. Paul's."

Replied the rector: "I suppose it's not the first time anybody ever talked about underwear in St. Paul's, but it's surely the first time anybody ever talked about underwear from the pulpit at St. Paul's!"

Alden Aaroe was buried under a tree in Richmond's Hollywood Cemetery, a place overlooking the James River and holding the remains of many legends in the long and storied history of the city. Only family and Aaroe's closest friends attended the burial service.

He was buried wearing a suit jacket, a white dress shirt, a necktie, and his favorite pair of blue jeans.

The white shirt's pen pocket has a large ink stain, because Aaroe's pens always were leaking in his pockets.

His underwear is a Millard the Mallard T-shirt, his favorite pair of University of Virginia boxer shorts, and socks imprinted with Valentine's hearts.

Tucked away in the casket are a trick pool ball, a deck of cards, a small transistor radio and a headphone set, a wooden box with several nuts, bolts, screws and a link of chain, and a yellow carpenter's ruler -- broken.

Items in his coat pockets include one small bungee cord, a family photograph, a photograph of the farm house in New Jersey, and a short piece of string.

There is one other special item in the casket. It is a twig from a white pine tree that grows by the pond on Tim Timberlake's property, a tree that took root several years ago when Alden helped Tim plant some cuttings from a white pine on Alden's property.

Alden Aaroe's legacy lives on in many wondrous ways.

Chapter Twelve

a.

b.

c.

a. Anna Petersen Aaroe, Alden's mother, referred to in the family as
    Anna P.
b. The Petersen family farm house, in Oxford, N.J., probably taken
    before Alden was born.
c. A family outing, from left: Alden's mother; his grandfather, Peter,
    who was known as Poppa; his cousin Faye; his grandmother
    Christeane Janny, and Alden.

As Alden would have said, "Just sittin' and thinkin'."

b.

a.

c.

a. The fascination with airplanes began on a visit to the Chicago World's Fair in 1933.
b. Swimming with best friend, Karl Alfred, in Summit, N.J.
c. High school graduation picture in 1936.

a.

b.

c.

a. In the stands for a football game at the University of Virginia.
b. At the University the year he lived on East Range across from the
   Med School.
c. In costume for a Virginia Players production.

On a remote broadcast for WCHV at the Charlottesville train station,
1941, waiting for the first diesel train to come through town. Alden is
the tall one on the right.

a.

b.

c.

a. Cadet Alden P. Aaroe, U.S. Army Air Forces, 1943.
b. Lt. Aaroe in Ft. Sumner, New Mexico., Spring 1943.
c. Alden in front of the Edna Kay in Tripoli, Libya.

a.

b.

a. Alden and Anna Lou, April, 1946, in the yard on Ridge Road.
b. Alden, Edna and Anna Lou, September 1946.

Alden talking backstage with Sunshine Sue at the Old Dominion Barn
Dance which was broadcast by WRVA.

a.

b.

a. A very early promotional photo at WRVA. Wasn't he handsome!
b. Alden interviewing Bob Hope for the Streetman Street Man Show on the corner of 5th and Broad. This is when Hope called him the man in the gutter.

a.

b.

c.

a. The "Little House" as originally built in 1947.
b. The "Little House" with the added living room, porch and garage in 1951.
c. Alden with his wheelbarrow full of treasures in front of the garage. The garage was always so full of tools and projects that no car was ever parked there. The wheelbarrow has survived and was a Christmas gift to Anna Lou several years ago.

a.

b.

c.

a. A green English Crosley was his first second car. Alden named it "Petit Chou," French for little cabbage. How did he ever fit in it?
b. The "Big House" completed. That car is Mr. Morris. Sheppy is in the driveway.
c. Alden in his typical work clothes with a borrowed tractor.

a.

b.

a. For about six months in 1957, Anna Lou went to work with her father on Saturday mornings. She did terrible things like play Elvis Presley records.

b. Camping at Cape Hatteras in the late 50's with the trailer, tent, tarp and assorted gear.

Recording an interview with John Whitten, a chicken farmer. Aaroe
discusses broiler production with producer Whitten, a sucessful raiser
for many years who was one of the thousands of the farm listeners to
the Aaroe show.

a.

b.

a. The big board at the studios on Church Hill. Alden was very proud that he ran it by himself for so many years. It was fascinating to watch him do a 4 1/2 hour show cueing, timing, flipping switches, answering the phone and talking all at the same time.
b. Alden with his new partner, Tim Timberlake, in 1985.

a.

b.

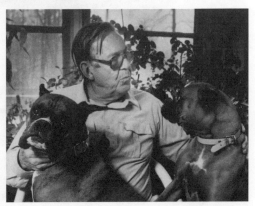

c.

a. Alden and Anna Lou in 1992.
b. Happy Poppa Bear with his rascally grandchildren, Karen and
   Andrew Willet, Christmas 1992.
c. Alden with his beloved boxers, George and Cleo.

a.

b.

c.

a. Alden and Virginia Governor Doug Wilder both received honorary degress from the University of Richmond in 1990.
b. The 75th birthday party at WRVA, Alden and Frances.
c. Same day, John Tansey hugs his "most famous hire."